JOSEPH RAO

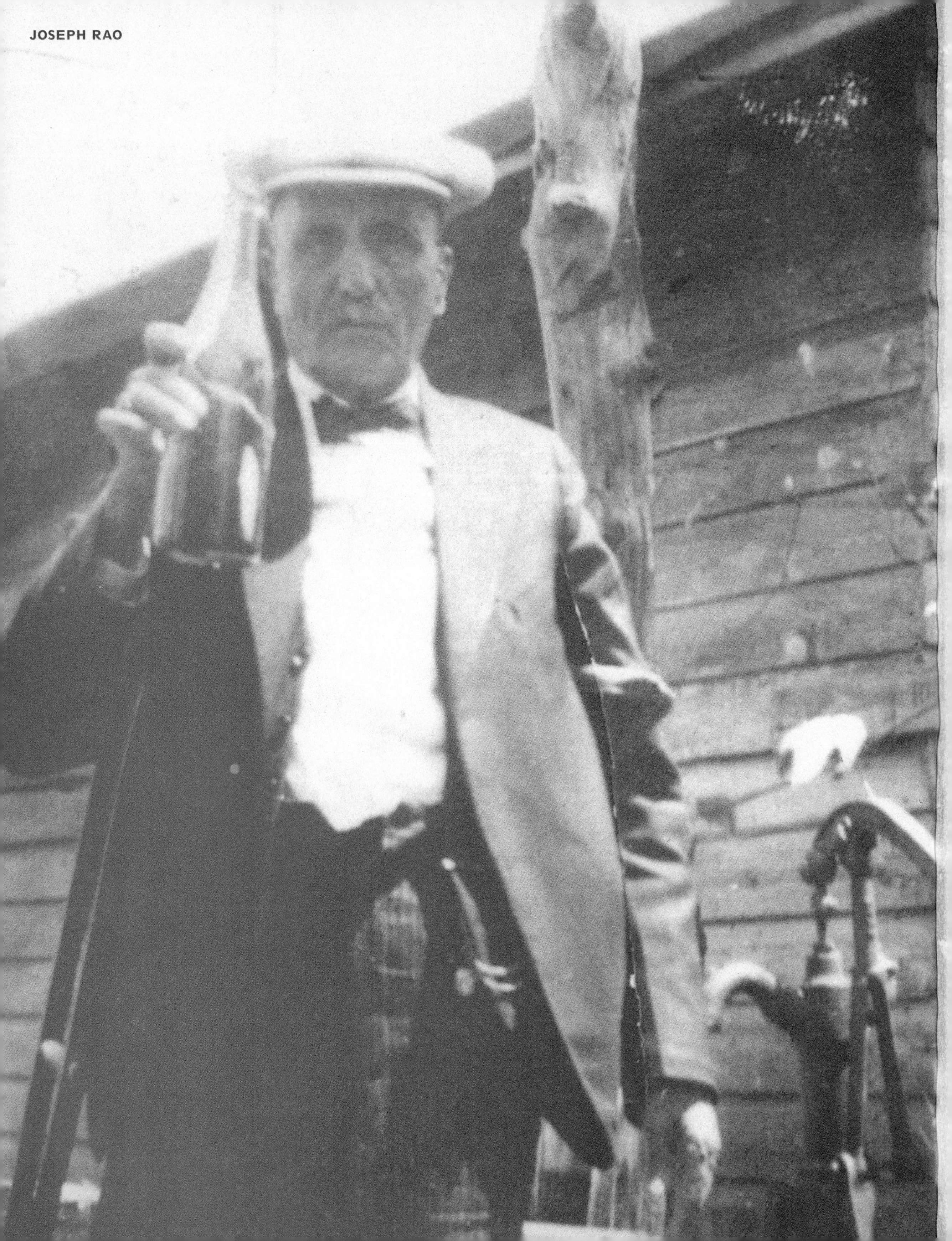

RAO'S COOKBOOK

RAO'S COOKBOOK

Over 100 Years of Italian Home Cooking

FRANK PELLEGRINO

Preface by Dick Schaap

Introduction by Nicholas Pileggi

Photographs by Stephen Hellerstein

and from the Rao's family album

RANDOM HOUSE 🏠 NEW YORK

Library of Congress Cataloging-in-Publication Data
Pellegrino, Frank.
    Rao's cookbook : Over 100 years of Italian home cooking / Frank Pellegrino, with an introduction by Nicholas Pileggi.
        p.   cm.
    Includes index.
    ISBN 0-679-45749-6
    1. Cookery, Italian.   2. Rao's (Restaurant)—History.
    I. Pileggi, Nicholas.   II. Rao's (Restaurant)   III. Title.
    TX723.P346   1998
    641.5'097471—dc21   97-34543

Random House website address: www.atrandom.com
Printed in the United States of America on acid-free paper
25 24 23 22

Book design by Georgiana Goodwin

Photos by Stephen Hellerstein: pages i, ii–iii, vi–vii, viii, ix, xi, xvi, xvii, xviii–ix, xxii, 3, 6, 10, 13, 14–15, 16, 19, 20, 24–25, 27, 30–31, 36, 40–41, 46, 49, 54, 57, 58, 68–69, 71, 75, 77, 78–79, 80, 83, 86, 88–89, 94, 105, 108, 109, 112, 115, 116, 118–19, 124–25, 127, 131, 134, 136–37, 139, 141, 149, 152–53, 154, 156–57, 160, 163, 164–65, 166, 168–69, 172
Photos by Hiro: pages 146, 147

Special thanks to Nick LaMicela and Frank Pellegrino, Jr., for their creative contribution

This book is dedicated to

the memory of Vincent

and

Anna Pellegrino Rao —

without you

there would be no Rao's

CONTENTS

MAMMA JAKE

PREFACE

DICK SCHAAP

I am a typical New Yorker. I don't own a car. I don't own a house. The only thing I own of value is my Monday night table at Rao's. I know what's important.

I started going to Rao's in the 1970s. The first time—and only the first time—was by accident. I had been city editor of the New York *Herald Tribune* in the 1960s. I thought I really knew the city. After all, I hung out in Harlem with Malcolm X, in Greenwich Village with Lenny Bruce, on the Lower East Side with narcotics cops and heroin addicts. I used to walk around Manhattan, look up at the buildings, and say, only half kidding, "This is my city."

I was wrong. I didn't know the city. I didn't know Rao's. I had never heard of the joint.

Then Mike Burke, a good guy who'd run the New York Yankees and Madison Square Garden and, I think, the circus, who'd been a war hero big enough to be played in a movie by Gary Cooper, decided he was going to retire, leave town, and move to Ireland.

Jimmy Breslin, the newspaperman, my oldest friend, my first boss—he was nineteen and I was fourteen—and I and our literary agent, Sterling Lord, wanted to take Burke out for a farewell dinner. We told Mike to pick the place. He chose Rao's, and I have been grateful ever since.

Even before we finished our meal—the best meal I'd ever eaten—I was asking what I had to do to whom in order to get a reservation. In those days, it wasn't impossible to get a table. It was just incredibly difficult. Frankie Pellegrino, then the maître d', captain, and waiter for all of the eight tables, told me I could have a reservation after the seasons changed.

Eventually, by behaving well and tipping better, I worked myself up to a table once a month. You can't imagine how proud I was when I was promoted to every other week. And, finally, a table every Monday. I was a regular. I was made. "If you want to get a table at Rao's," the food critic Gael Greene wrote in *New York* magazine, "you have to know one of two people." I was one of the two. I hadn't been so proud since Richard Nixon, upon being elected president of the United

States, chose two hundred new books for the White House library, and only two authors were represented by as many as three books: Bruce Catton and me. *A Stillness at Appomattox* shared the president's shelves with *Instant Replay.*

Everyone wanted to share my table at Rao's. Many offered to buy it from me. I think I could have sold my four chairs each Monday for enough to become a regular at Le Cirque. I couldn't do that. I did the next best thing. People said, "Let me eat dinner with you, and I'll pick up the tab," and I let them. I even let them talk sometimes. Of course, I wasn't able to go to Rao's every Monday—sometimes, I was out of town on assignment; sometimes, I was trying to diet—so I would give the table away to friends and relatives. My son Jeremy and my daughter Michelle thought that using the table in my absence was the highest form of bonding. My wife offered our table to her hairdresser and her chiropractor, figuring it would improve her hair and her back. I lent the table to Steve Palermo, the umpire, who shared it with David Cone, the pitcher. I also lent it to Walter Anderson, the editor of *Parade,* who shared it with Jerry Lewis, the actor.

Among the people I've brought to Rao's are Phil Simms, Billy Crystal, Bo Jackson, Patti LuPone, Tom Seaver, Mary Carillo, George Brett, Bill White, Chris Dodd, and Martina Navratilova. No one ever left hungry, or disappointed. The ones who caused the most excitement were Simms and White. Simms had been the Most Valuable Player in the Super Bowl a week before he popped up in Rao's; when Johnny Roast Beef, whose acting career had not yet flowered, saw Simms walk in, he got up, drove out to New Jersey, and brought his son back to get Simms's autograph. Bill White, a black man from Ohio, was treated like a king at Rao's, not because he once played baseball for the New York Giants but because, as a broadcaster of New York Yankee games, he worked with Phil Rizzuto, "the Scooter," a treasure to the Italian Americans who came out of East Harlem.

Rao's appeals to all the senses, of taste and smell, sound and sight. The seafood salad is so fresh it swims to your table; the escarole and beans duel for control of the soup they flavor. The conversations you overhear may be haunting or hilarious, and if you want to stare at beautiful people, you can pick John Kennedy, Jr., or Robert Redford, Sharon Stone or Brenda Vaccarro, depending on your age and sexual inclination.

But Rao's greatest appeal is to a different sense, to my sense of the absurd. You can wear a tuxedo to Rao's, or jeans, and feel equally comfortable. You see Ron Perelman sitting at a booth, backed up against an ex-cop at the next booth. You see Mariah Carey and Beverly Sills sitting at adjacent tables, and you wonder how you can coax them into a duet. You see Joe Biden, the Delaware Democrat, sharing pasta with Al D'Amato, the New York Republican, and you wonder what brings such political opposites together. "I can't help it," Biden says. "I like Italian food."

I will never forget the night that Billy Crystal and I went to Rao's to celebrate finishing writing his autobiography, *Absolutely Mahvelous,* and we looked around and realized that Roy Cohn was

The first time I went to Rao's was with my good friend Dick Schaap of ABC Sports. To my left was the notorious Roy Cohn, who, ironically, was eating something with a red sauce. He was a little drunk, muttering to one of his shrimp, "Are you now or have you ever been a member of the crustacean family?" On the other side was Claus von Bulow, who was going over the galleys of his book with his editor. He had also consumed a vat of Chianti before his appetizers. His editor said, "Claus, that should be a comma . . ." Claus laughed and said, "You mean coma, don't you?" and laughed a sardonic laugh. I turned to Mr. Schaap and said, "I love this place!"

BILLY CRYSTAL

P.S. Not many people order the sliced steak, but trust me, it's great.

sitting at a table on one side of us and Claus von Bulow was sitting at a table on the other side. We thought we had died and gone to hell. But we were at Rao's, so we knew we were in heaven.

Another time, my wife and I were eating with a friend from *The New York Times* and his wife, and during the course of dinner, a prominent New York politician came over to our table and said, "How do you like this place? Isn't it terrific? I love it. I've never been here before."

He went back to his own table for fifteen or twenty minutes, then visited us once more. "How do you like this place?" he said. "Isn't it terrific? I love it. I come here all the time."

I haven't the slightest idea which time he was telling the truth. I think he was lying just for practice.

One of the lures of Rao's is its speakeasy past, the suspicion that every other diner is the God-father of something or other. Of course, the odds are that the six guys in dark suits just came from a golf match in New Jersey, not from a sit-down, but still the scent of the underworld adds to the glamour of Rao's. Once, I was eating with a friend, a former New York City homicide detective, who seemed unable to concentrate on his meal. "What's the matter?" I asked.

"See that guy back there?" my friend said. He nodded in the direction of a man seated near the back wall.

"Yeah?"

"He's a bad guy."

"Who is he?"

"I don't know," the ex-cop said. "I can't remember. But I know I interrogated him sometime. He's a bad guy."

The presence of the bad guy ruined my friend's meal, and when the bad guy finished his dinner and, on his way out, walked past our table, he suddenly stopped, looked at me, and said, "Dick, how are you?"

At that point, I recognized him. He was a perfectly legitimate guy who had worked with Joe Namath in the 1960s at Joe's bar, Bachelors III.

It is true that John Gotti has eaten at Rao's.

It is not true that he has eaten there lately.

Rao's has to be the only restaurant in the world that displays photographs of Woody Allen (inscribed, "Please turn this picture to the wall") and a belly dancer and Pope John Paul II. Two of the three are autographed, and two of the three are occasional customers. If the Pope wants to make a pilgrimage to Rao's, he won't have to wait four months for a table. Frankie is willing to make exceptions to the rules for all people who are popes, or higher.

Remarkably, in the more than two decades that my wife and I have been patronizing, and delighting in, Rao's, only twice have we forgotten to use the Monday night table, bestow it on a friend, or turn it back to Frankie for his use. The first time, I suddenly remembered my gaffe the following day, while I was sitting with friends in Lawrence, Kansas.

When I called New York, I found out that Rao's had burned down Sunday night. Frankie would never have known that I had missed my reservation.

The second time was a couple of years later.

I remembered at about nine o'clock Monday night while I was eating dinner in an inferior restaurant in Atlanta. And I remembered what had happened the last time I failed to cancel.

I rushed to the phone and called Rao's number.

I could not have been happier when I heard a familiar voice answer.

Rao's had survived my absence.

Introduction

NICHOLAS PILEGGI

The Rao family arrived in New York from the southern Italian town of Pollo, near Naples, in the 1880s and settled amid the scattering of shacks and tenement buildings that were then beginning to sprout up in East Harlem. The area in those days was filled predominantly with Irish and German immigrants, but by the turn of the century the Italians, recruited in work gangs as laborers for the city's new water, sewer, and subway systems, began to arrive in unprecedented numbers.

Charles Rao was a child when his mother and father arrived in New York, which meant he grew up with the distinct advantage of speaking English at a time most of the immigrant Italians were still struggling with the language.

A bright and resourceful young man, Charles Rao bought a small saloon from the George Ehret Brewery at the corner of 114th Street and Pleasant Avenue in upper Manhattan. It was 1896. He called the place Rao's.

In those days, most of the large breweries would buy up corner properties and sell them at bargain rates to saloon keepers who sold the brewer's beers. Long before six-packs and refrigerators, draft beer for home consumption was sold directly from a bar's taps. Around dinnertime, customers would come to the saloon with tin beer pails. Sometimes they would smear grease or oil around the inside lip so that the pail would not be filled up mostly with foam. Rao's was one of the few bars that had pewter pipes installed so that the beer—carried from the wooden casks in the cellar to the spigots at the bar—kept its taste and was always cold.

Charles Rao died in 1909 of a heart attack, and his brother Joseph took over and ran the restaurant until his death in 1930. By then Charlie's sons Louis and Vincent Rao had become the operating owners. A third Rao brother, Joseph, best described as a Damon Runyon sort of guy, had very little to do with the running of the restaurant.

Louis and Vincent kept the bar open during Prohibition. One of the neighborhood families, the Caianos, made their own wine in their cellar next door, and it was pumped into Rao's basement through a hose. Rao's sold the wine for a dollar a bottle.

Louis Rao, in his Chesterfield topcoats and white-on-white shirts, was, by neighborhood standards, very suave. He had his hair cut by his regular barber way downtown at the Waldorf-Astoria. He traveled extensively during the age of steamships, and when his mother, Francesca, died, he had to return from Egypt. While overseeing the bar, Louis did not allow swearing or ungentlemanly behavior, and he was more than capable of tossing obstreperous customers onto Pleasant Avenue.

Louis ran the place until his death in 1958; then his brother Vincent took over. Vincent Rao was a very different kind of man. Instead of tailored clothes and Waldorf haircuts, Vincent Rao preferred a cowboy hat and casual clothes. He also preferred cooking to bossing around customers. He didn't travel the world; he rarely left the block. He was born in 1907 in the house next door to the bar, 453 East 114th Street. He was raised in that house, he was married in that house, and he died in that house, at age eighty-seven, in 1994.

In the first part of the century, East Harlem occupied a thirty-square-block area filled with tenements. First Avenue was lined with pushcarts. Italian food stores sold macaroni in bulk and lined their walls with the glistening golden gallon cans of imported olive oil. Fish stores sold dried cod, or baccalà, stacked like cords of firewood near the door, and bushels of snails, baskets of live crabs, and barrels of eels were always available. Cheese stores made their own mozzarella in the mornings and it was bought warm; the ricotta was so fresh it had to be sold in tall tin cans with holes in them to drain away the excess water. Loaves of freshly baked bread—both long and round, with seeds or without—came out of neighborhood bakery ovens two or three times a day, and a family dinner was rarely eaten without warm, fresh-baked bread.

These stickball neighborhoods were pockets of great social stability. Despite the poverty, the five-story walkups, the absence of decent schools, and the garbage that often littered the streets, these communities confounded city planners and social engineers for generations. The people who lived in them hated to leave. The first Italian parish church in the city, Our Lady of Mount Carmel, was built in 1884 on 115th Street, and it became the center of a thriving Italian immigrant community and sponsor of a popular religious feast that attracted huge crowds who devoured the sausage sandwiches, fried squid, fresh clams, and anchovy zeppole sold on the streets. The neighborhood was full of Italian artisans—masons, bricklayers, carpenters, tile men—and nobody ever wanted to move. As late as the mid-1950s and early 1960s, when many of the first- and second-generation residents were making more than enough money to buy into the suburban American dream, Italian American neighborhoods were still largely intact. The local residents had been unaffected by real estate developers and gentrification. At one time or another, they successfully fought off improved public housing, overhead expressways, indoor pushcart markets, and packaged white bread. Even the urban ravages of drugs and crime were not enough to dislodge many of the neighborhood residents. In fact, street crime rates in these neighborhoods remained low despite their general increase in other parts of the city.

For years, neighborhoods like East Harlem followed a code of social behavior based much more on the codes of small, remote, nineteenth-century southern Italian villages than the laws of most of the city's residents. Parking regulations, strictly enforced elsewhere in the city, were almost totally disregarded. Vendors sold ices, broiled sausages, and offered pony rides for children without city permits. Sidewalk cafés opened without licenses. Fire hydrants were used indiscriminately for neighborhood summertime showers, and shoveling snow and sweeping sidewalks were more a matter of whim than law. Pushcarts blocked streets and garbage was burned at the curb while bookmakers and numbers runners took bets with very little municipal interference. Neighborhoods like East Harlem and Mulberry Street lasted as long as they did because they remained socially frozen, like the Calabrian and Sicilian villages upon which they were based.

But by the 1970s, the neighborhood that had so long resisted change finally succumbed.

For the first half of this century, East Harlem probably had a larger concentration of Italian Americans than any other section of the city. Our Lady of Mount Carmel Church was built by the artisans who lived in the neighborhood. Starting in 1884, these craftsmen, who had come to New York to help build the city, started working on their own church during their spare time and days off.

"For years, Our Lady of Mount Carmel in East Harlem was the principal Italian church in the city," says its pastor, Father Peter Rofrano. "The attention has always been focused on the life-size statue of Our Lady of Mount Carmel, which was crowned by Pope Pius X on July sixteenth, 1904. We have reports that on the day of her coronation, tens of thousands of people marched behind the statue of the Madonna as she was carried through the neighborhood."

That July 16 procession continued to grow until, by the mid-1950s, the ten-day Our Lady of Mount Carmel feast was one of the largest religious festivals anywhere in the country, and thousands of pilgrims would follow the Madonna's statue as it was carried through East Harlem. In those days, some of the most devout followed the procession in bare feet. Others would carry long wax models of afflicted limbs and various body parts for which they needed divine intercession.

There was also more than a touch of carnival mixed in with the religious theme of the feast, and the neighborhood was filled with lights erected on fifty-foot poles, food stalls, calliope music, kiddie rides, and tables with gambling games.

During those years, Our Lady of Mount Carmel had about fifty thousand Italian American parishioners living in the neighborhood. Today, according to Father Rofrano, there are fewer than five hundred.

The thriving Italian East Harlem neighborhood is long gone, and Rao's is one of the few places holding the neighborhood's fading memories together.

It was Vincent who turned Rao's from a local bar—a place neighborhood people used to call "the Hole" because it was (and is) four steps down from the street—into a restaurant where customers began to return even after they moved out of the neighborhood. Vincent loved food. He loved to cook. He especially enjoyed grilling steaks and chops and chicken on a charcoal grill he set up on the street right outside the entry. The first Rao's regulars returned primarily for Vincent's steaks and chops.

By 1974, business had become so brisk that help was required in the form of Vincent's wife, Anna Pellegrino Rao, who arrived from their house next door with her pots and recipes. Anna was an unlikely restaurant chef. She was as elegant as her husband was homespun. Her look included a slim figure, a long gold cigarette holder, tightly upswept white-blond hair, white cashmere slacks and turtlenecks, gold sandals, monogrammed tinted glasses, and a single strand of pearls. When longtime regular Woody Allen made *Broadway Danny Rose,* he based Mia Farrow's look on Anna Rao's distinctive appearance. Anna's deft touch improved all the traditional Italian dishes, and Rao's became a favorite for a small army of steady customers.

Over the years, Rao's has probably survived because its owners have refused to change. They did not expand by filling the floors above the kitchen with additional tables, as they were advised. In the late sixties and early seventies, when the East Harlem neighborhood began its decline, Rao's did not move downtown, as was suggested by many of its customers. As a result, Rao's has become a sort of time-capsule restaurant that allows its customers to dip back into an earlier period and experience a neighborhood restaurant as it was.

So after dozens of glowing reviews, and even after the addition of movie stars, corporate moguls, politicians, and sports figures (who are usually brought as guests of Rao's regulars), it is the original Rao's customers who fill the limited number of tables every night.

Because of Rao's out-of-the-way location, when a customer walks down the four steps, the scene looks more like a stage set than a normal restaurant. On the left is a view of the bustling open kitchen, but once you enter the dining area, the mood changes. The low stamped-tin ceiling, the soft wattage of the overhead lamps and wall sconces, the darkly varnished booths, the canopied bar with its tinsel lights and perpetual Christmas decorations, are all very relaxing. Since every chair at every table for the night has been assigned, there is no anxiety at the bar about jockeying for a next "available" table. The background music is provided by Rao's jukebox (*New York* magazine declared it one of the ten best in the city), and it's stocked with hours of Sinatra, Dinah Washington, the Ink Spots, and Tony Bennett.

Because so little—in the way of food, decor, and customers—has changed over the years, Rao's has a rare neighborhood authenticity. As the *Zagat Survey* points out, on any given night at Rao's, you could be sitting next to a governor or a Godfather.

More likely, of course, the *Zagat* diner will be sitting next to a judge or a businessman, but the neighborhood's history as a mob stronghold, which dates back to Prohibition, lends at least the illusion of authenticity. It was at dinner one night, for instance, that Martin Scorsese cast at least six of the roles in his film *GoodFellas* from restaurant regulars, including ex-cop Bo Dietl; Johnny "Roast Beef" Williams, who ran a delicatessen at the time; and Frankie Pellegrino himself, who played "Johnny Dio" and can be seen frying steaks in a prison scene.

Despite its extraordinary success, Rao's is still a cash-and-carry neighborhood joint, closed for lunch and weekends, and with only one seating per table a night.

"That's why it doesn't matter what time you get here," Frankie says. "Seven o'clock or nine o'clock, your table waits for you."

Anna and Vincent were determined not to change the place according to the restaurant industry's fashion of the day. It meant that they were never going to make as much money as they might have, but they thought of the restaurant as an extension of their home and enjoyed the fact that they knew just about every guest at every table every night.

For twenty years, it has not been easy to have dinner at Rao's. It wasn't easy before then, either: Rao's is a tiny place, and its regular customers keep the place filled to capacity. But on the morning of August 19, 1977, *New York Times* restaurant critic Mimi Sheraton wrote a glowing three-star review of the restaurant, and it became so hard to get a table there that—as the *Zagat Survey* recently put it—even the Pope would find it tough.

"Mimi Sheraton would come with a couple of regulars, and they would always order lots of dishes so that she could taste different things," Frankie Pellegrino recalls. "We never knew who she was until one night, as her group was leaving, she stopped by the kitchen, which has no door and is right at the entrance, and introduced herself to my Uncle Vincent.

"She said that she was from *The New York Times* and that she would like to write something about the restaurant. If you knew Vincent Rao, you knew that he did not care much for publicity. He cared about his place. He cared about his friends from the neighborhood who would come in and spend the night. He was happy with the place the way it was. He wasn't interested in making it any more than that. The restaurant was like his home, and he and his wife, my Aunt Anna, enjoyed cooking and talking with the regulars.

"So when Mimi Sheraton tells Vincent, who was seventy years old at the time, that she's going to review the restaurant in *The New York Times,* he smiled, thanked her, and held up his thumb and index finger about an inch apart and said, 'Please, keep it small.' "

She wrote half a page.

All during the night following the appearance of the *Times* review, the telephone rang. Vincent and Anna went about their cooking and paid no attention. Frankie spent the night explaining to callers that Rao's was a very small place with a limited number of tables and that most of them were already taken on most nights by regular neighborhood customers. He also explained that there was no second seating, that the restaurant wasn't open on weekends, that they did not take credit cards, and that there was no lunch service.

"At the end of that night," Frankie says, "the phone was still ringing, but we all thought the noise and hoopla would blow over. It was a Friday. We were closed Saturday and Sunday, and best of all, we were going on vacation for three weeks. We'd be gone. Who would remember three weeks from now? There would be other restaurant reviews, and people would go chasing after other reservations, and we could go back to living normal lives."

Any hope that things would return to normal after the vacation evaporated when everyone returned to work. Getting a table at Rao's would never be the same. The problem presented by the Mimi Sheraton review was purely mathematical. There was simply no way a restaurant like Rao's, with eight tables already occupied by regulars, serving one meal per night per table, could possibly accommodate a newspaper readership numbering in the millions.

"But now," says Frankie, "the calls just kept coming in, and I began to think that maybe this was all pointing us toward a grand opportunity. Maybe it was time to expand. There were three empty floors above the restaurant. My uncle and aunt owned the whole building. Why not expand?

"I explained it all to Vincent and Anna. We could break through the walls of the storeroom in the back and add a few tables. I had a friend who was an architect. We started looking at bearing walls. We started discussing plans. But Vincent said no. Instinctively, he knew that you couldn't really change this place and keep it the same. This is Rao's. You change it and it is no longer Rao's. For a while back then I didn't understand, but now I do."

So the family did nothing. The restaurant did not change in any way. The regular customers who had been occupying the same tables on a Monday or Tuesday or Wednesday night for years continued to occupy them. In fact, to this day, no matter how many movie stars, corporate moguls, politicians, and sports figures have found their way to the restaurant's scarce tables, the original customers take up most of the space.

In 1997, twenty years after Mimi Sheraton, Annie Sausto, who was working the day Sheraton's review appeared, is still in charge of opening the restaurant door at nine in the morning and checking the day's deliveries. It's not a long commute for Annie, a childhood friend of Vincent and Anna Rao. She still lives on East 114th Street, where she was born in 1917.

By midafternoon, just as he did the day the review appeared, Nicky "the Vest" Zaloumis arrives with the sausage. "I got my nickname a few years ago when people started giving me vests," Nicky says. "I wear a different one every night."

By late afternoon, the kitchen is ready for the cooks.

The bread still comes from the G. Morrone Bakery on 116th Street between First and Second avenues, and the meat from Dominick Loiacono, the butcher.

The mozzarella, prosciutto, pancetta, and the grating cheeses all come from Mario's Delicatessen, which, not surprisingly, is on Second Avenue, next door to Dom's Meat Market on 115th Street. The fish and calamari for the fish salad come from Pisacane's fish store, at 940 First Avenue.

There have been some changes since the Sheraton review. About fifteen years ago, Peter LaPadura, a Rao's regular and old friend who was born and raised in East Harlem, brought in one of his mother's cheesecakes. Being Rao's, slices of Petey's mother's cheesecake were soon being distributed around the restaurant.

Today, Petey's mother, Rose, turns out five cheesecakes a week for Rao's. That's one a night. Experienced diners learn to place their cheesecake orders the minute they sit down, before it's sold out.

As a result of the restaurant's unique concept of customer "table rights," Rao's is probably the only certifiable condominium restaurant in the world. The tables are essentially owned by the customers.

The Rao's regulars all know one another so well that there has been a market established in Rao's tables. "We trade tables like baseball cards," Bo Dietl says. "I'll give you Thursday for Monday."

The juggling and assigning of these rarely available tables occupies much of Frankie's time.

"I know that the way things are we have our problems about getting everyone a table," Frankie says, "but at least when they do get in, everything is the way it always was and the way Anna and Vincent always wanted it to be."

FROM THE AUTHOR

For twenty-five years I have been trying to figure out what Rao's is all about. I give up. I can't. Many years ago the neighborhood people called it The Hole because you have to walk down four steps to the entrance. My Aunt Anna and Uncle Vincent called it The Saloon. I call it The Joint. It's all of the above. It's none of the above. It is itself, its own entity. It lives. It breathes. It communicates better than you and I can. It talks straight to your soul. It provokes you. It makes you remember. It makes you relate. It makes you realize how lucky you are to have people to love and to share with. It lets you know that the simple things in life are the best and most important. A good meal, a good friend, a good conversation: That's as good as it gets in this world. And in its own magical and mystical way, the room that is known as Rao's tells you that.

One night, a young man named Joe was sitting at the bar. I could see that he was taking it all in, trying to figure it out. I sat down next to him and asked, "How's everything going, Joe?"

He turned to me and said, "Frank, you know what the difference is between Rao's and every other restaurant?"

Naturally I said, "Tell me, Joey."

"Every other restaurant you leave, you leave full," he said, patting his stomach for emphasis. "Rao's you leave fulfilled." This room, known as Rao's, talked to him.

Rao's is over one hundred years old. Same location, same room, same family. The ceiling is tin. The walls are dark wood paneling and marble. The floor is dark stained oak. The bar is dark oak paneling with a red leatherette bar rail. The booths are made of wood; the tables are covered with white linens. There is a red canopy over the bar with Christmas decorations. There is a statue of the Madonna in the front window.

For over one hundred years, this room has been inhabited by unique people, one-of-a-kind people, incredibly interesting people. How did they find their way to this room? Why? Why am I a part of this room? I don't know. I do know that this room has absorbed every thought, every feeling, every emotion, every word, every value, every tradition, of everybody who has been in it for the past one hundred years. It sorts out the best of it and then carefully and joyfully parcels out its wisdom to anyone willing to listen. This room has touched many lives in many, many positive ways—many of which I am not even aware of, yet I know this to be true.

Writing this introduction was more difficult for me than you might imagine. Putting feelings into words is not always that simple. I do not know how to describe "magic" or define "incredible." Sometimes these things are best left alone—you know it when you see it, however it is you see it, and that should suffice. My sincerest hope is that this book, which emanates from this room called Rao's, brings a smile to your heart as well as to your palate.

Frankie

Few among those who go to restaurants realize that the man who first opened one must have been a man of genius and a profound observer.

—BRILLAT-SAVARIN

Over a century ago, genius and profound observation collided in Harlem—resulting, however, not in a restaurant but in an institution. From humble beginnings on seemingly sacred ground, the intimate eatery at 114th Street and Pleasant Avenue would burgeon into one of the most storied restaurants in New York City lore, and it would bear the family name Rao's. Steeped in history, shrouded in mystique, Rao's is where luminaries from sports, politics, and entertainment—as well as the indigenous denizens of East Harlem—all fit under one roof and share in the most inimitable dining experience in New York.

A few of the guys are huddled around a transistor radio, anxiously awaiting the score from the Yankees game; the senator at table 2 is plotting his reelection strategy; the lady in the booth down the back has four platinum albums to her credit; a table of eight has just broken into spontaneous song, bolstering a Drifters classic coming forth from the jukebox . . . and it's only Monday night. No wonder a reservation is a virtual impossibility. "The Book," as it is called, contains the names of the fortunate ones, as reservations now become available on a biannual basis. If you like a place with easier admission, try Harvard.

Rao's is quintessential New York. Replete with character, attitude, and swagger, with a heart as big as its host city and an authenticity that has made it the standard bearer of Italian dining. So while other establishments bend to fads and indulge the mercurial whims of what is fashionable, Rao's will brave the new millennium, sans TV or PC, under the scrupulous stewardship of the same family that opened its doors over a hundred years ago. In an attempt to unearth the enduring appeal of Rao's, one might look to the fact that they aren't open for business on weekends, they don't accept reservations by phone, and they have no menus . . . just like home.

JOSEPH RICCOBENE

THE LAST OF THE STEEL MAGNOLIAS

Annie
Of the gravel voice
At once soft and hoarse

Annie of the cashmere turtlenecks
And high-heeled mules

Annie
All in white

An ever-present cigarette
Burning bright

Elegantly inhaled
Through an ivory holder

Smoke like a halo
Drifting about her upswept
Blond hair and shoulders

Annie
Keeper of secrets
Of food and family
Secrets
Of lemon chicken
Of long engagements
And all the years in between . . .

Annie
Four stars
To our Rao's
Queen

A final toast
With a glass of white wine
To a woman
Of few words
A legend in her own time

Love, loyalty, and
A whispered goodbye

Above, now, with Vincent
East Harlem's last wish

Annie
We'll miss you
Pleasant Avenue blows you a kiss. . . .

—Christina Krauss

("Good night, Annie, thank you.")

Aunt Anna's Kitchen

Stocked with the same products that my family has used for generations, the kitchen at Rao's is really quite simple. The finest canned plum tomatoes (pelati), certified "San Marzano," imported from Italy; first-rate imported dried Italian pastas (known affectionately as macaroni); fine-quality pure olive oil (we use Filippo Berio); Italian-style red wine vinegar; crusty Italian bread from Morrone on 116th Street; fresh garlic; homemade vinegared peppers; fresh mozzarella cheese; freshly grated Pecorino Romano and Parmigiano-Reggiano cheeses. That's about it!

We buy our meat, fish, fruit and vegetables, cheeses and bread, fresh daily from our neighborhood stores. You should do the same! Search out local purveyors who specialize in Italian products and are knowledgeable about Italian tradition. You will almost always be able to select produce that is garden-fresh and products that are of high quality and frequently homemade as well. Neighborhood shopping gives you the opportunity to become friendly with the store employees, who can direct you to the market's best. Perhaps you might have to spend a few cents more, but I know that you will find those extra cents repaid with great taste and a genuine Italian homemade feeling.

Back in the Rao kitchen, right next to the stove, we keep the night's supply of Flavored Olive Oil (see page 10), clam juice, Chicken Broth (see page 8), lemon mixture for chicken (see page 81), and broccoli rabe water (see page 138).

Each day, we prepare our salad vegetables, the vegetables for the night's sauté, Roasted Peppers (see page 17), our homemade Bread Crumbs (see page 11), and, of course, our Marinara Sauce (see page 5). The routine is not much different from what my uncle and my aunt did and what many southern Italian immigrant families still do at home. It is this consistency that has kept our meals never-changing and ever deliciously homemade.

Marinara Sauce

Salsa Marinara

At Rao's, we use our Marinara Sauce on all kinds of pasta, as well as a major component in many other dishes. Each morning, Annie Sausto makes a huge pot of fresh sauce to get us through that night's service. We never have any left over. The imported tomatoes that we use come flavored with basil (basilico), but we always add additional fresh basil for its pungent aroma and taste. In the early days, our sauce was made from fresh tomatoes in the summer and home-canned in the winter. Today, I think nothing could be better than the canned, imported San Marzano tomatoes we use all year. The most important step is to clean the tomatoes of all skin and to remove the hard part of the core—this is what makes our sauce so smooth.

MAKES APPROXIMATELY 7 CUPS

2 28-ounce cans imported Italian plum tomatoes with basil (preferably those labeled "San Marzano")

¼ cup fine-quality olive oil

2 ounces fatback or salt pork, optional

3 tablespoons minced onion

2 garlic cloves, peeled and minced

Salt to taste

6 leaves fresh basil, torn, optional

Pinch dried oregano

Pepper to taste

1. Remove tomatoes from the can, reserving the juice in which they are packed. Using your hands, crush the tomatoes, gently remove and discard the hard core from the stem end, and remove and discard any skin and tough membrane. Set aside.

2. Put oil in a large, nonreactive saucepan over medium-low heat. If using fatback, cut it into small pieces and add to the pan. Sauté for about 5 minutes or until all fat has been rendered. Remove and discard fatback.

3. Then add onion. Sauté for 3 minutes or until translucent and just beginning to brown. Stir in garlic and sauté for 30 seconds or until just softened (see Note). Stir in tomatoes, reserved juice, and salt. Raise heat, and bring to a boil. Immediately reduce heat to a very low simmer and cook for about 1 hour or until flavors have combined and sauce is slightly thickened. (If you prefer a thicker sauce, cook for an additional 15 minutes.)

4. Stir in basil, oregano, and pepper, and cook for an additional minute. Remove from heat and serve.

Notes: Take care when adding garlic to hot oil, as it will burn and turn bitter very quickly. If this happens, discard oil and vegetables and start again.

We never have sauce left over; however, if you do, store it, tightly covered and refrigerated, for a day or two or freeze for up to 3 months.

I've been a customer and friend of Rao's for many years, having one memorable meal after another. I always looked to Annie Rao as the consummate businesswoman and chef.

As she walked the dining room, she said hello to everyone, but sat down with only a handful of people, like T.J., Angelo, Louis D., and Frankie. When she did sit down, she would light up a cigarette and put it in her ever-present cigarette holder.

I was eating there one night when Annie passed and said hello. I said, "Annie, when are you going to tell me how to make your marinara sauce?" With that one question, she spent the next fifty Thursday nights trying to make a chef out of me. We would critique what and how I cooked the previous week. She would soften my mistakes with a laugh. Either the oil was too hot or not hot enough; the garlic was to be minced, not sliced. She became a great friend, and I miss her dearly.

Now when I'm at Rao's I can still see her great smile in the kitchen and dining room. I feel a special love for her, and I know she loved me, too. She guides my hand every time I stir the sauce.

JIMMY "CIGARS" LACERRA

BROTHS

Brodi

We know that professional chefs call these stocks, but to us, they are just "brodi," or broths. They are always necessary to make good Italian soups and are frequently served simply as health-reviving light broths to which some pastina or bits of chicken, meat, or cheese, and parsley have been added. Our brodi serve as core ingredients for many of our dishes and we continue to make them just as Uncle Vincent's mother did.

MEAT BROTH

Brodo di Carne

MAKES APPROXIMATELY 2 QUARTS

2 pounds beef or veal shinbones, cracked

1 large beef or veal knuckle bone

1 pound lean beef or veal meat, bottom or
   top round

2 plum tomatoes, quartered

2 leeks, chopped

2 stalks celery, chopped

1 large onion, peeled and chopped

1 large carrot, peeled and chopped

2 tablespoons minced Italian parsley

1 bay leaf

1 teaspoon whole peppercorns

Approximately 4 quarts cold water

Salt to taste

1. Preheat oven to 400°F.

2. On a baking sheet with sides, roast bones and meat for about 20 minutes or until lightly browned, with some fat rendered out. Drain off the fat and set bones and meat aside.

3. Put tomatoes, leeks, celery, onion, carrot, parsley, bay leaf, and peppercorns in a large stockpot with 4 quarts cold water over high heat. Add salt and bring to a boil. Add browned bones and meat. Bring back to a boil, then lower heat and simmer gently, uncovered, for about 3½ hours, skimming off the scum as the broth cooks. Remove from heat and let rest for 30 minutes.

4. Line a colander with cheesecloth or a double layer of paper towels. Drain broth and discard bones and vegetables. Strain broth again through a fine sieve lined with cheesecloth.

Cool in an ice water bath before refrigerating or freezing. When cool, remove congealed fat. Store, covered, in 1- to 2-cup portions for convenient use. The broth can be refrigerated for up to 3 days or tightly sealed and frozen for up to 6 months.

CHICKEN BROTH

Brodo di Pollo

MAKES APPROXIMATELY 2 QUARTS

6 pounds chicken necks, backs, and wings

2 leeks, chopped

2 stalks celery, chopped

1 plum tomato, quartered

1 large onion, peeled and chopped

1 large carrot, peeled and chopped

2 tablespoons minced Italian parsley

1 bay leaf

1 teaspoon whole peppercorns

Approximately 4 quarts cold water

Salt to taste

1. Preheat oven to 400° F.

2. On a baking sheet with sides, roast the chicken pieces for about 15 minutes or until brown, with some fat rendered out. Drain off all fat.

3. Put leeks, celery, tomato, onion, carrot, parsley, bay leaf, and peppercorns in a large stockpot with 4 quarts of cold water. Add salt and bring to a boil. Add browned chicken pieces and return to a boil, then lower heat and simmer gently, uncovered, for about 3½ hours, skimming off the scum as the broth cooks. Remove from heat and let rest for 30 minutes.

4. Line a colander with cheesecloth or a double layer of paper towels. Strain broth and discard chicken and vegetables. Strain broth again through a fine sieve lined with cheesecloth. Cool in an ice water bath before refrigerating or freezing. When cool, remove congealed fat. Store, covered, in 1- to 2-cup containers for convenient use. The broth can be refrigerated for up to 3 days or tightly sealed and frozen for up to 6 months.

There are few invitations that bring a bigger smile to the faces of my friends and business associates than when I ask, "Would you like to join me at Rao's for dinner?"

It's truly incredible how people react when they hear that they will have a chance to eat at Rao's.

Great food, a fun atmosphere, and friendship. That's Rao's, and you can't beat it.

RUSTY STAUB

VINEGARED HOT CHERRY OR SWEET BELL PEPPERS

Peperoni Sott'Aceto

Every Italian family has a special pickling brine for vegetables. We use this one to preserve peppers that add zesty flavor to dishes such as Chicken Scarpariello (see page 87). You also can purchase vinegared hot cherry peppers and sliced sweet peppers at Italian markets, specialty food stores, and some supermarkets.

MAKES 1 QUART

1 pound hot red cherry peppers or 1½ pounds red or yellow bell peppers

6 tiny pickling onions

1 tablespoon coarse salt

Approximately 2 cups white wine vinegar

Approximately ½ cup cold spring water

1. Wash and dry peppers. Leave cherry peppers whole, with stems attached. Core, quarter, and seed bell peppers. Remove all membrane and cut into ½-inch-thick strips. Set aside.

2. Peel onions and cut an *x* into both ends. Add to the peppers.

3. Fill a 1-quart canning jar with boiling water and let stand for 1 minute. Drain water and immediately pack cherry or bell peppers and onions into the jar, sprinkling with salt as you pack.

4. Pour vinegar over peppers and add water, if needed, to cover peppers completely.

5. Tightly seal jar and shake well to mix. Place in a cool, dark place to marinate for at least 2 weeks before using.

Note: You can also pickle onions, cauliflower, artichoke hearts, and eggplant in this brine.

FLAVORED OLIVE OIL

MAKES 1 CUP

1 cup fine-quality olive oil (such as Filippo Berio)

4 garlic cloves, peeled and crushed

1. Heat oil in a small, heavy saucepan on medium-low heat. Add garlic and barely simmer until garlic is just beginning to brown. Remove and discard garlic. Pour oil into a clean container and reserve, at room temperature, to use as flavored oil for frying and sautéing.

SEASONED EGG BATTER

This is a Rao's secret! You will find that our Seasoned Egg Batter adds authentic Italian gusto to mildly flavored meats and fish in preparations such as Veal Milanese and Fried Fillet of Sole. Begin with the best-quality meat or fish, dip in flour, then in this batter, and, finally, in homemade bread crumbs. Fry it up for a real Rao-style treat!

MAKES ENOUGH TO COAT 1½ POUNDS OF MEAT OR FISH

4 large eggs

¼ cup freshly grated Pecorino Romano
   cheese

2 teaspoons minced Italian parsley

Salt and pepper to taste

1. In a small bowl, whisk eggs, cheese, parsley, salt and pepper vigorously until well blended. Use immediately as a batter for breaded meat or fish.

BREAD CRUMBS

Unless you make your own bread crumbs, you won't be following Rao's kitchen tradition. Use the finest-quality Italian bread you can find (we have been using Morrone from 116th Street in Manhattan for generations) and allow it to dry for at least two days. Then grate, using a handheld grater or a food processor fitted with the metal blade. Shake and push the bread crumbs through a medium strainer to get an even texture. And, remember, as Aunt Anna Rao used to say, "The better the bread, the better the crumbs."

Store, tightly covered and refrigerated, for no more than 1 week.

PREPARING GARLIC

Every day, we use many cloves of fresh garlic. To make them easier to peel, we soak them in a bowl of warm—not hot—water for at least 15 minutes before easing off the paper-thin skins. We leave some cloves whole and we push others through a garlic press, ready to be added to soups or sautés.

Cooking Dried Beans

Before cooking, dried beans must be presoaked in ten times as much water as beans for, at the minimum, 4 hours, preferably 8.

Discard soaking water and place beans in a large saucepan with cold water (or unsalted broth) to cover by at least 2 inches. Bring to a boil over high heat. Lower heat and simmer for about 1½ hours or until tender, adding liquid as necessary so that the beans have a nice, rich broth. Do not add salt or any acidic liquid or vegetable to uncooked beans, as these ingredients will toughen them. To be safe, add all seasonings after beans have softened.

If you do not have time to prepare dried beans, canned beans, particularly cannellini beans, kidney beans, and chickpeas, are most often of excellent quality. Do not hesitate to replace home-cooked beans in any of our recipes with canned beans.

A Note About Vinegar

We use Italian-style red wine vinegar for salad dressings and seasonings. We all love its tangy flavor. Occasionally, we use the more recently available aged balsamic vinegar imported from Italy to cook with.

If God said, "You can choose only one cuisine," I'd say, "Italian." If She asked what my favorite restaurant was, I'd say, "Rao's."

LINDA GRAY

APPETIZERS

I go to Rao's for special occasions, whether it is dinner with my children or if I want to offer someone an unforgettable evening.

We usually arrive after 9:00 and are warmly received by Frankie. He seats us at a booth with a white tablecloth. Nicky, who runs the bar and makes the best martinis in New York, offers us a drink and immediately cracks open a bottle of Italian red wine.

Soon afterward Frankie junior pushes up a chair and catches me up on Rao's news.

I always order for the table and rarely deviate from my favorites. Then Frankie goes through the menu and tries to get me to change my routine and order fewer pastas and more main courses. Then his face breaks out into a smile and he writes down the steady order: peppers, fusilli with filetto di pomodoro sauce, rigatoni with broccoli rabe and sausage, lemon chicken, large salad.

Before the food arrives, I make a pilgrimage to the jukebox and put on a medley of great jazz and blues.

The peppers arrive at room temperature with a sweet taste from the white raisins.

Soon after, Anthony brings us the two pastas and serves them family style. He then brings over a shaker of parmesan and a shaker of hot red peppers. The pastas are always perfect. They are cooked al dente and never have too much sauce.

By the time the lemon chicken arrives, Rao's has transplanted me to a relaxed time and place where everyone is part of a family. Half the restaurant is joining Frankie in a Dean Martin song or we are lost in quiet conversation, having forgotten that we are in New York. This could be Italy or another era.

The lemon chicken is crispy and tangy. The salad is fresh and light.

Then it is cigar time and I quietly light up. Nicky offers us a drink on Frankie.

Another unforgettable night at Rao's.

ALEXANDER VREELAND

ANTIPASTO

"Antipasto" means nothing more than "before the meal"—a little something to quiet the hunger pangs while you wait for the main event. Never meant to be a filling part of the meal, antipasto should just whet the appetite. At Rao's, we feature only a few specialties, just as our grandmothers did at home; it was only on very special occasions that platters of antipasti preceded our meal. However, when requested, we will prepare a cold antipasto platter featuring prosciutto, salami, mozzarella, hard-boiled eggs, Roasted Peppers (see page 17), anchovies, broccoli spears, and Gaeta olives.

If you choose to prepare an antipasto platter, you might combine some excellent prosciutto with various types of salami, cheese, grilled vegetables, marinated artichoke hearts, Roasted Peppers, Seafood Salad (see page 21), olives, and vinegared vegetables (see page 9). I have not provided you with a recipe, as I feel that antipasto should allow each cook some creativity. If you are preparing a special-occasion meal, antipasto is the perfect dish to introduce the theme of your dinner.

Roasted Peppers

Each day, Annie Sausto prepares a batch of 40 to 50 peppers. The smoky aroma fills the restaurant and lingers until serving time. Always marinated and served at room temperature, our peppers are never held over from one day to the next, as we feel that freshness ensures their homemade taste.

FOR 6 PEPPERS

6 red bell peppers

½ cup fine-quality olive oil

3 tablespoons golden raisins

2 tablespoons pine nuts

1 teaspoon chopped Italian parsley

⅛ teaspoon minced garlic, optional

Salt and pepper to taste

1. Preheat broiler.

2. Broil the peppers, turning frequently, until skin has blackened on all sides. Remove from broiler and immediately put into a large brown-paper bag. Seal tightly. Allow peppers to steam in the sealed bag for about 20 minutes or until cool enough to handle.

3. When peppers are cool, remove from bag. Remove the blackened skin, stems and seeds, and cut the peppers, lengthwise into ¼-inch-thick strips.

4. Let strips stand in a colander for at least 3 hours or until most of the moisture has drained off.

5. Combine peppers with oil, raisins, nuts, parsley, and, if using, garlic. Season to taste with salt and pepper and stir. Allow to marinate for at least 1 hour before serving at room temperature.

Rao's: what is there left to be said about that magic room with its ten tables (after ninety-nine years they added two tables last year)? I daresay there is scarcely a luminary in the entertainment or business galaxy who has not appeared, or sought to appear, at that tiny restaurant in the middle of East Harlem. I will name-drop shamelessly and say I have sat within feet of Ron Perelman, Billy Crystal, and Sharon Stone with Robert Goulet singing a cappella at the bar. Not unusual. Rao's size, of course, is what dictates its exclusivity. And the attendant denial of entrée to major players, of all stripes, has only served to heighten the legendary aura about the place. But however unique (one hundred years on the same corner), the never-failing warmth and conviviality of Rao's renders it world-class on the ambience scale. That, as we say in the law, is beyond cavil.

The food? I am no gastronomic prodigy, but given a choice I might well order my last meal from there, certainly to include the roasted peppers, the secrecy of whose formula is on a par with the Manhattan Project.

Rao's, que viva!

EDWIN TORRES

Mozzarella in Carrozza

SERVES 6

6 slices Italian bread, about ½ inch to ¾ inch thick

6 bread-size slices fresh mozzarella, cut ¼ inch thick

1 cup all-purpose flour

1 recipe Seasoned Egg Batter (see page 11)

2 cups Bread Crumbs (see page 11)

Approximately 3 cups Marinara Sauce (see page 5)

Approximately 6 cups vegetable oil

2 tablespoons chopped Italian parsley

1. Trim crusts from bread. Put each mozzarella slice on top of bread and trim to fit.

2. Dredge both sides of each piece of bread and cheese in flour. Shake off excess. Set aside.

3. Put Seasoned Egg Batter in a shallow bowl and Bread Crumbs into a second shallow bowl. Dip each piece of bread and cheese into the Seasoned Egg Batter, then into Bread Crumbs, pressing lightly to coat well. Set aside, in a single layer, on a plate until ready to fry.

4. Warm Marinara Sauce in a small, nonreactive saucepan on very low heat.

5. Heat oil in a deep-fat fryer to 350° F (the usual deep-fry temperature, 365° F, is too hot for the delicate brown this requires). Fry mozzarella-and-bread pieces two at a time for approximately 1 minute or until golden. Remove from oil and drain on paper towel.

6. Spoon ½ cup of warm Marinara Sauce onto each of 6 warm plates. Put one Mozzarella in Carrozza in the center. Sprinkle with chopped parsley and serve.

Variations:

1. Whisk together 4 large eggs. Dip mozzarella-and-bread pieces into flour, then into the beaten eggs. Again, dip into flour. Press into grated Pecorino Romano cheese (about 1 cup totally). Fry as above.

2. Place a slice of prosciutto between the bread and cheese. Do not use prosciutto with cheese-coated variation above as the combination will be too salty.

If you do not have a deep-fat fryer, place about ½ inch of vegetable oil in a heavy sauté pan over high heat. When the oil is very hot but not smoking, add mozzarella-and-bread pieces, without crowding, and fry for about 1 minute per side or until golden. Continue as above.

SEAFOOD SALAD

Frutti di Mare

Perhaps the most popular dish at Rao's is our Seafood Salad. I think that this is because the simplicity of the dish epitomizes and underscores the premise of all Rao's cooking. Putting together this salad, I realized that, in an abstract way, it could very well serve as a definition of Rao's. The varied yet individually unique seafood ingredients represent the diversity of our customers. The simple and delicate sauce, which is the perfect complement to the rich seafood, represents our philosophy of simplicity in cooking. And the refreshing manner in which the ingredients meld together represents the fusion of attitudes that creates the comfortable, welcoming ambience of the restaurant.

At Rao's, we do not marinate our Seafood Salad as we feel that if it is allowed to stand, the lemon juice will "burn" the mild seafood and the garlic overwhelm the subtle flavor. Of necessity, we do prepare the components ahead of time, but each salad is made to order. You should adjust the oil, lemon, and garlic to your own taste. Even in our kitchen, we have a continuing "more lemon—less oil" versus "more oil—less lemon" debate.

SERVES 6

1 pound fresh, small squid (calamari) with tentacles, cleaned (see Notes)

2 cups lemon juice

4 tablespoons salt

8 large shrimp

1 cup fine-quality olive oil

2 garlic cloves, peeled and halved

1 teaspoon chopped Italian parsley

Salt and pepper to taste

1 cup jumbo lump crabmeat

1 pound cooked fresh lobster meat

6 lemon wedges

1. Rinse squid in a colander under cold running water. Separate bodies and tentacles, as they must be cooked in different water to keep the tentacles from coloring the rings.

2. Place about 1 quart cold water in a medium pot. Add squid bodies, ¼ cup fresh lemon juice, and 2 tablespoons salt.

3. Place about 1 quart cold water in a medium pot. Add squid tentacles, ¾ cup fresh lemon juice, and 2 tablespoons salt.

4. Bring both pots to a rolling boil. Lower heat to a gentle boil and cook until squid are very tender, about 5 minutes.

5. Remove from heat and run cold water directly into each pot until water is cool.

6. Drain the bodies, pat dry, and cut into rings.

7. Holding the tentacles, run warm water into the pan. Under the running water, gently rub between the palms of your hands, pushing the black specks and colored skin from the tentacles. Drain well and pat dry.

8. Combine the rings and tentacles in a colander. Cover with a damp cloth and set aside to drain for about 20 minutes. Refrigerate if not using immediately.

9. Peel, devein, remove tails, and butterfly shrimp (see Note). Cover with water and bring to a boil in a small saucepan. Immediately remove from heat, drain, and refresh in cold, running water. Gently press in a clean kitchen towel to dry well. Cut into quarters. If not using immediately, cover with a damp towel and refrigerate.

10. In a nonreactive bowl, whisk together the oil, remaining lemon juice, garlic, parsley, and salt and pepper to taste.

11. Add shrimp and squid to the oil mixture. Toss to coat. Using a slotted spoon, remove seafood from oil mixture and place on a serving plate.

12. Add crabmeat to oil mixture and very gently turn to coat. Using a slotted spoon, remove crab from oil mixture and gently fold into the shrimp-squid mixture.

13. Add lobster to the oil mixture. Gently toss to coat. Using a slotted spoon, remove lobster from oil mixture and place on top of salad. Discard garlic from oil mixture. Pour remaining oil mixture over salad and serve immediately, garnished with lemon wedges.

Notes: When purchasing fresh, whole squid always look for those that are clear-eyed, smooth-skinned, and very fresh-smelling. Have the fishmonger clean and cut the squid to your specifications. Some fresh squid are sold precut into rings with the tentacles removed; however, the rings and tentacles are usually sold together. As the squid cooks, skim off the foam that accumulates at the top.

To butterfly shrimp, peel and devein, leaving the tail on for most preparations and removing it only when called for in a specific recipe. Using a sharp knife, make a shallow cut from head to tail along the center but not through the shrimp and remove the dark vein. Lay the shrimp open, deveined side up, and make shallow cuts diagonally out from the center on both sides.

Handle the crabmeat carefully so that the lumps remain whole. However, do check for cartilage and shell remnants.

Baked Clams Oreganate

SERVES 6

36 fresh littleneck, small cherrystone or
   manilla clams (2 to 2½ inches)

2 cups Bread Crumbs (see page 11)

½ tablespoon minced Italian parsley

⅛ teaspoon minced garlic

½ to 1 teaspoon dried oregano (see Note)

Salt and pepper to taste

½ cup fine-quality olive oil

¾ to 1 cup Chicken Broth (see page 8)

6 lemon wedges

6 sprigs Italian parsley

1. If you don't know how to open clams yourself, ask a fishmonger to open them for you, leaving them on the half shell. Refrigerate until ready to use.

2. Place broiler tray on the lowest rack and preheat broiler.

3. Combine Bread Crumbs, parsley, garlic, oregano, and salt and pepper. Add olive oil and toss mixture until crumbs are evenly coated. Add the broth and continue to mix until very well blended. The mixture should be quite wet.

4. Put approximately 1 heaping teaspoon of bread-crumb mixture on each clam. Smooth over the top, making sure that the edges are sealed. Using the edge of a teaspoon, cut ridges into the topping.

5. Pour ⅛ inch cold water into cookie sheet with sides (to keep the clams moist while broiling) and broil for about 7 minutes or until the bread-crumb topping is well browned and crisp.

6. Put 6 clams on each of 6 small, warm serving plates. Garnish each plate with a lemon wedge and parsley sprig and serve.

Note: This dish requires a definite oregano taste, so you should sample as you add the herb, keeping in mind that dried oregano varies tremendously in intensity.

I have read the Bible, I have read The Longest Day, *I have read the life of Caruso. This book is the life of good food.*

PAT COOPER

Soups and Salads

Fresh Clam Zuppa

Zuppa di Vongole

SERVES 6 TO 8

---

36 fresh littleneck, small cherrystones or
    manilla clams (2 to 2½ inches)

¼ cup Flavored Olive Oil (see page 10)

3–4 garlic cloves, peeled and mashed

1 35-ounce can imported San Marzano
    Italian plum tomatoes, well drained and
    crushed

4 cups bottled clam juice

½ cup dry white wine

½ teaspoon dried oregano

Crushed red-pepper flakes to taste

One sprig fresh basil, or 4 or 5 leaves

Salt and pepper to taste

1 tablespoon chopped Italian parsley

1. Rinse the clams under cold water. Put in a colander to drain off excess water.

2. Heat oil in a large, heavy saucepan over medium heat. Add garlic and sauté one minute until golden but do not allow to burn. Add clams.

3. Add tomatoes, clam juice, wine, oregano, and red-pepper flakes. Raise heat and bring to a boil, then lower to a steady simmer and cook for about 7 minutes or until liquid begins to reduce.

4. Cover and continue to cook for about 5 minutes or until all clams have opened. Stir in basil and salt and pepper.

5. Toss in parsley and pour into warm, shallow soup bowls, allowing 6 clams per serving. Serve hot with lots of warm, crusty bread to soak up the delicious sauce.

Note: Discard clams that do not open. They may be bad or they may be "mudders." Of course, "mudders"—mud-filled, clamless shells—will not open during cooking and many northwestern clams will stay determinedly closed even after a long period of cooking.

By adding extra clam juice and eliminating the tomatoes, this zuppa can be made white instead of red.

I can't remember ever having anything except a wonderful meal and a wonderful time at Rao's. When Aunt Anna was in the kitchen, she always managed some special dish that I had never tasted before.

But my fondest recollection was the night I gave a dinner for the benefit of the New York Public Library. The motif was the Prohibition era, and all the ladies came dressed as flappers. In front of each plate was a miniature bathtub with a miniature bottle of gin in it that my friend Christy Ferer had provided. But the surprise came when an actor dressed as a policeman "raided" the restaurant and "arrested" me for illegal possession of booze. It was a great party and could only have happened at Rao's.

BEVERLY SILLS

Escarole and Beans

Scarola e Fagioli

SERVES 6 TO 8

½ cup fine-quality olive oil

1 garlic clove, minced

4 cups cooked cannellini beans (see page 12)

1 cup bean broth or Chicken Broth (see page 8)

2 large bunches escarole, cooked and chopped (see page 140)

Salt and pepper to taste

Freshly grated Pecorino Romano cheese, optional

1. Heat oil in a large saucepan over medium heat. Add garlic and sauté for 2 minutes.

2. Stir in beans. Then add broth, escarole, and salt and pepper. Lower heat and cook for about 5 minutes or until hot, adding additional broth if you prefer a thinner soup.

3. Serve with a sprinkle of Pecorino Romano cheese, if desired.

Pasta and Peas

Pasta e Piselli

SERVES 6 TO 8

1 pound tubetti or other small macaroni

½ cup olive oil

⅓ cup diced onion

½ cup diced prosciutto

3 cloves garlic, peeled

2 15-ounce cans tiny young peas with their liquid, or 2 cups cooked fresh peas

Salt and pepper to taste

Freshly grated Pecorino Romano cheese, optional

1. Place macaroni in rapidly boiling, salted water and boil until al dente. Drain, reserving about 1 cup pasta cooking water.

2. While pasta is cooking, heat olive oil in a sauté pan and stir in the onion, prosciutto, and garlic. Sauté over medium heat until onion is translucent, approximately 3 minutes. Set aside.

3. When pasta is cooked al dente, add peas, with their liquid, to the pasta water. Stir to heat through. Drain the peas and pasta, reserving 1 cup of cooking water. Return peas and pasta to pot and add reserved cooking water. Add contents of sauté pan and stir over medium heat for 1 minute. Serve with a sprinkling of cheese.

PASTA AND BEANS

Pasta e Fagioli

SERVES 6 TO 8

½ cup fine-quality olive oil

1 cup diced onion

⅓ cup diced prosciutto or pancetta

2 cloves garlic, peeled

4 cups cooked beans with 1 cup of their cooking liquid (see page 12) or 2 15-ounce cans Great Northern or cannellini beans with their liquid

4 cups Chicken Broth (see page 8)

Salt and pepper to taste

2 cups canned imported San Marzano Italian plum tomatoes, well drained and chopped

1 pound tubetti or other small macaroni, cooked (see page 42)

¼ cup freshly grated Pecorino Romano cheese, optional

1. Combine oil, onion, prosciutto, and garlic in a large saucepan over medium heat. Sauté for about 5 minutes or until onions are translucent and begin to turn golden. Do not burn garlic.

2. Stir in beans and their liquid. Add broth and salt and pepper and bring to a boil. Add tomatoes and return to a boil. Lower heat and simmer, uncovered, for 10 minutes.

3. Stir in pasta and cook for an additional 5 minutes. Serve hot, sprinkled with Pecorino Romano cheese, if desired.

Note: You can eliminate the tomatoes for a rich, creamy soup; however, you might need to add additional bean or chicken broth if you prefer a thinner soup.

PASTA AND CHICKPEAS

Pasta e Ceci

SERVES 6 TO 8

1 cup diced pancetta

4 garlic cloves, peeled

1 cup diced, canned, imported San Marzano
Italian plum tomatoes

4 cups cooked chickpeas with 1 cup of their
cooking liquid (see page 12) or 2 15-ounce
cans chickpeas and their liquid

6 cups Chicken Broth (see page 8) or water

¾ pound small, tubular macaroni or broken-
up pieces of spaghetti or fedelini, cooked
al dente (see page 42)

Salt and pepper to taste

Freshly grated Pecorino Romano cheese,
optional

1. Sauté pancetta in a large saucepan over medium heat for 5 minutes or until just crisp.
Add garlic and sauté until lightly golden. Stir in tomatoes and bring to a boil.

2. Add chickpeas and their liquid and return to a boil. Add broth and macaroni and return to
a boil. Lower heat and season with salt and pepper. Simmer for 5 minutes or until flavors are
well combined. If desired, remove garlic cloves before serving.

3. Serve hot, sprinkled with cheese, if desired.

There are few perfect experiences in life, and one happens to be dinner at Rao's. This cannot be attributed merely to the food, which is sublime in the way perfect home-cooked Italian food can be sublime. No, the experience of Rao's is the experience of a kind of profane epiphany—an epiphany available perhaps only in New York. Somehow, it's always Christmas there, only better. It's as if Christmas were not only a sacred feast but an infinitely charming Italian opera, set in a darkly glowing room with twinkling champagne lights, four booths, a jukebox, and a bar. Once inside, the conviction arises that nothing can go wrong, and in fact nothing ever does. Frank Pellegrino may be the last great maître d' in New York, the way Rick was the last great maître d' in Casablanca, and he presides with much the same deftly self-deprecating worldliness, irony, and charm. On any given night the restaurant's dramatis personae present a distillation and intensification of New York: regulars (not to be confused with locals); locals; celebrities; heavies; politicians; hotshots; family. Indeed, the culture of Rao's, like the culture of New York itself, is both sui generis *and absolutely inconceivable anywhere else. Like the city's great institutions, but on a smaller scale—like Central Park, for example, or Grand Central Station, or the Virgin of 115th Street just around the block—Rao's seems to exist in a world of its own; a world where the glamorous and the ordinary, the miraculous and the everyday—the world the way we wish it were and the world the way it is—for a brief moment jubilantly converge. If this seems a somewhat exalted way of describing a place to eat, go there sometime.*

RIC BURNS

Pasta and Lentils

Pasta e Lenticchie

SERVES 6 TO 8

---

1 pound lentils, well washed and drained

3 large carrots, peeled and diced

3 stalks celery, tops off, peeled and diced

1 cup diced onion

6 garlic cloves, peeled

½ cup fine-quality olive oil

1½ tablespoons chopped Italian parsley

1 teaspoon dried oregano

Salt and pepper to taste

¾ pound fedelini, broken into 1- to 2-inch
  pieces, cooked al dente (see page 42)

¼ cup freshly grated Pecorino Romano
  cheese, optional

1. In a 6-quart saucepan, combine lentils, carrots, celery, onion, and garlic. Add water to cover plus two inches. Stir to blend.

2. Add oil, parsley, oregano, and salt and pepper. Bring to a boil.

3. Lower heat and simmer for about 30 minutes or until lentils are just tender.

4. Stir in the pasta and bring to a boil. Boil for 1 minute. Serve, sprinkled with cheese, if desired.

Note: Fedelini can be replaced with ditalini or rice.

When I first visited Rao's—many moons ago, before the fire—I had heard from Michael Bell, an L.A. actor friend, that I must go to eat there when I went to New York. He knew the chef at the time and said, "Here's her number. Try to get a reservation; it ain't easy." It was a very busy restaurant, following the old, steadfast credo in New York: fiercely loyal to old friends and best customers. I finally understood why: They take care of you like family.

BRENDA VACCARO

MINESTRONE

SERVES 6 TO 8

½ cup fine-quality olive oil

1 cup chopped onions

1 cup chopped whole leeks

¼ cup minced Italian parsley

1 teaspoon minced fresh thyme

2 cups peeled and diced potatoes

2 cups diced carrots

1 cup diced celery

1 cup diced zucchini

1 cup fresh fava beans

1 cup fresh or frozen green peas

2 cups canned imported San Marzano Italian plum tomatoes, with juice

4 cups Chicken Broth (see page 8) or water

Salt and pepper to taste

1 to 2 cups cooked cannellini or kidney beans (see page 12)

2 tablespoons chopped fresh basil

¼ cup freshly grated Pecorino Romano cheese

1. Heat oil in a large stockpot over medium-high heat. When hot, stir in onions, leeks, parsley, and thyme. Lower heat and sauté for about 5 minutes or until onions begin to brown.

2. Add the remaining vegetables—potatoes, carrots, celery, zucchini, fava beans, and peas—one at a time, sautéing each for about 3 minutes. When all the vegetables are sautéed, stir in tomatoes, broth, and salt and pepper. Bring to a boil. Then lower heat and simmer for about 1 hour, until soup is quite thick.

3. Add cooked beans, mashing some against the side of the stockpot with the back of a spoon as you stir them in. Cook for an additional 5 minutes. Remove from heat and stir in basil. Serve sprinkled with Pecorino Romano cheese.

My friends have been part of Rao's way before it became a social must. I'd come to eat and hang out, leaving with a fat belly only my mother could duplicate.

After many years in California I came back to see my pals, and there's Christie Hefner sitting at one table and David and Gladice Begelman at another. I duck outside to see if I'm in the right joint, and Frank comes out, laughing. "You're in the right place, Burt. You've just been away too long."

Now, years later, Frank's a respected actor and Nicky still runs the bar; the food is still great (theirs is the only bottled sauce I'd take home), and whoever's left is still here to make me feel at home.

BURT YOUNG

Rao's Simple Mixed Green Salad

I have more requests for this recipe than for any other. Yet when I tell folks how to make it, they return with: "Mine didn't taste like it does in the restaurant." I think this is because people tend to add much more vinegar than we do. But, remember, it is really all a matter of personal taste.

SERVES 6

1 medium head iceberg lettuce

1 small head radicchio

1 head endive

2 medium, very ripe tomatoes

1 small cucumber

½ cup finely sliced fresh fennel

¼ cup finely sliced red onion

¾ cup fine-quality olive oil

1 to 2 tablespoons red wine vinegar

Salt to taste

1. Core lettuce and radicchio. Soak in a sink filled with cold water for about 5 minutes. Tear apart and dry thoroughly. Set aside in a large salad bowl.

2. Pull endive apart and wash and dry well. Cut into pieces and add to salad bowl.

3. Peel and core tomatoes. Cut in half, crosswise; then cut each half into quarters. Toss into lettuce mixture.

4. Peel cucumber and cut, crosswise, into thin slices. Toss into lettuce mixture.

5. Toss fennel and onion into salad.

6. Drizzle oil over salad, then sprinkle with vinegar. Add salt, toss to coat, and serve.

It was over several memorable dinners at Rao's that John Kennedy, Michael Berman, and I became truly inspired to launch George *magazine.*

DAVID J. PECKER

TOMATO AND RED ONION SALAD

Insalata di Pomodori e Cipolle

SERVES 6

6 to 8 very ripe tomatoes, washed, cored, and cut into 8 wedges each

1 cup fine-quality olive oil

3 tablespoons Italian-style red wine vinegar

2 large red onions, peeled and cut lengthwise into slivers

4 to 5 garlic cloves, peeled and minced

8 to 10 leaves fresh basil, torn

Salt to taste

½ teaspoon dried oregano

1. To tomatoes add oil and vinegar, then onions, garlic, basil, and salt. Toss to combine.

2. Spoon onto a well-chilled serving plate, sprinkle with oregano, and serve.

Note: For a heartier salad, overlap slices of fresh mozzarella on the serving plate. Spoon Tomato and Red Onion Salad on top and serve.

One of the nicest times I've had making a film was Broadway Danny Rose, *when I was able to help Mia create the female lead based on Frankie's Aunt Annie, who, along with her husband, ran the kitchen and did the cooking at Rao's. We copied her hairdo, her clothes, her dark glasses, her cigarette, and her wonderful sense of humor. I feel that I also contributed to Frankie's career as an actor. When I first met him, he was a waiter who wanted to be an actor, and I used him in several movies and was very impressed with what a terrific actor he is. Rao's is probably my favorite place to eat in New York, and I've had many exciting and romantic evenings there over the last decades.*

WOODY ALLEN

Insalata Tricolore

SERVES 6

2 bunches arugula, trimmed, washed, and
   dried

2 heads endive, washed, dried, and sliced

1 large head radicchio, washed, dried, and
   chopped

½ cup fine-quality olive oil

3 tablespoons Italian-style red wine vinegar

Salt to taste

1. Combine arugula, endive, and radicchio in a large salad bowl. Drizzle oil and vinegar over the salad and season with salt. Toss.

Broccoli Salad

SERVES 6

1 whole garlic clove, peeled

2 large heads broccoli, cooked (see
   page 141)

1 teaspoon minced garlic

½ cup of fine-quality olive oil

2 to 3 tablespoons fresh lemon juice or to
   taste

Salt and pepper to taste

6 lemon wedges

1. Using the whole garlic clove, rub interior of a wooden salad bowl.

2. Put broccoli in the bowl. Whisk together the garlic, oil and lemon juice then drizzle over the broccoli. Season to taste with salt and pepper, toss to combine, and serve with lemon wedges.

The only thing usual about an evening at Rao's is that there is never anything usual about an evening at Rao's.

BILL ROLLNICK AND NANCY ELLISON ROLLNICK

Uncle Vincent's Baccalà Salad

SERVES 6

2 pounds dried salt cod, cut into 3-inch pieces (see Note)

1 cup fine-quality olive oil

4 garlic cloves, peeled

⅔ cup fresh lemon juice or to taste

Pepper and salt to taste

2 cups Vinegared Hot Cherry Peppers or Sweet Bell Peppers (see page 9), halved and chopped

1 cup Gaeta olives

¼ cup salt-packed capers, well rinsed

2 tablespoons chopped Italian parsley

1. Soak the cod in cold water to cover in a cool spot for at least 24 hours or up to 3 days, changing the water frequently. After 24 hours, break off a tiny piece of fish and taste for saltiness. If fish is still quite salty, continue soaking until water is very clear and fish is almost sweet in taste.

2. In a large, heavy saucepan, bring approximately 6 quarts of cold water to a boil. Add cod and boil for 10 minutes or until fish easily flakes when poked with a fork. Drain into a colander, then lay fish on a platter to cool.

3. When cool, remove any skin and bones and break into bite-size pieces. Put fish in the center of a serving platter. Set aside.

4. Heat oil in a medium sauté pan over medium heat. Add garlic and sauté for about 3 minutes or until oil is nicely flavored and garlic is barely golden. Pour oil and garlic over the cod. Drizzle about half of the lemon juice over the top. Taste and add more juice as needed. Season with pepper and, if necessary, salt, taking care not to oversalt.

5. In a bowl, combine the vinegared peppers, olives, and capers then spoon over the seasoned cod. Sprinkle parsley over all and serve at room temperature.

Note: Dried salt cod may require up to 3 days of soaking to remove excess salt. In some Italian households, the soaking was done in constantly running cold water in the basement to keep the salted-fish smell out of the house. If it is properly soaked, the cooked fish will be sweet and fresh-tasting. Patience is truly a virtue here!

PASTA

COOKING DRIED PASTA

At Rao's, we use the segreto (secret) method to cook and serve dried pasta. It is the acknowledged proper way southern Italian women produce the best possible taste for their families.

Cook pasta in rapidly boiling salted water (about 4 to 5 quarts per pound of dried pasta) until "al dente" (slightly firm or "to the tooth"). Drain. Return pasta to the pot. Immediately stir in about ½ cup sauce (and, if desired, depending on the sauce, a few leaves of fresh basil, torn). Place over high heat and, using a wooden spoon, toss pasta and sauce together for about 1 minute. Pour into a large, shallow serving bowl or portion onto individual plates and top with additional sauce.

This method allows the cooked pasta time to absorb the sauce rather than letting the sauce simply coat the surface of the pasta. Additionally, you use less sauce, which allows you to really taste the flavorful pasta.

When choosing the type of pasta to use, keep in mind that thinner sauces (such as clam sauce) work best with thin, solid pastas, such as spaghettini or linguine, while thick, rich sauces marry best with large, hollow macaroni, such as rigatoni, which will hold on to any small pieces of meat or vegetables. Almost any pasta will work with marinara or other tomato-based sauces.

Penne with Tomato and Eggplant Sauce

Penne con Salsa di Pomodoro e Melanzane

SERVES 4 AS A MAIN COURSE • SERVES 6 AS A PASTA COURSE

1 cup olive oil

3–4 cloves garlic, peeled

1 1½-pound eggplant, cut into ½-inch cubes

8 large white mushrooms, sliced

½ cup chopped onion

Salt to taste

½ cup dry white wine

3 cups chopped, canned, imported San Marzano Italian plum tomatoes, with juice

Salt and pepper to taste

5 fresh basil leaves, chopped

Pinch dried oregano

1 pound penne

Freshly grated Pecorino Romano cheese, to taste

1. Put oil in a large sauté pan over medium heat. Sauté garlic until golden. Remove garlic. Add eggplant, mushrooms, and onions. Add salt and sauté for about 12 minutes or until vegetables are very soft and just beginning to brown, lowering heat, if necessary, to slow down browning.

2. Add wine and bring to a boil. Stir in tomatoes and return to a boil. Season with salt and pepper. Lower heat and simmer for 15 minutes or until flavors have blended. Stir in basil leaves and oregano and remove from heat.

3. While sauce is simmering, cook the penne in a large, deep pot in rapidly boiling salted water until al dente.

4. Drain penne. Return drained penne to the pot. Over medium-high heat, stir in ½ cup sauce. Using a wooden spoon, toss together for 1 minute. Remove from heat and pour into a large serving platter or bowl. Spoon remaining sauce over the top. Serve with a sprinkle of Pecorino Romano cheese.

Linguine with White or Pink Clam Sauce

SERVES 4 AS A MAIN COURSE · SERVES 6 AS A PASTA COURSE

3 dozen cherrystone clams, or 1 dozen cherrystone clams plus two 6½-ounce cans chopped clams (no preservatives added)

1 clove garlic, peeled and crushed

1 cup olive oil

1 cup reserved clam broth (see step 1, below) or 1 cup bottled clam juice

¼ cup dry white wine

Pinch dried oregano

1 pound linguine

10 sprigs parsley (leaves only), chopped

1 14-ounce can Italian tomatoes, drained and lightly hand-crushed (optional: for pink clam sauce only)

1. Scrub and wash clams under cold water. If using fresh clams, place 2 dozen clams in pot with ¼ cup water. Cover and bring to a boil; simmer until shells open. Remove clams (saving 1 cup of broth) and chop.

2. In a saucepan, sauté garlic in olive oil. When garlic begins to turn golden, add 1 dozen whole clams, along with the cup of clam broth and the white wine. Cover, and continue cooking, checking occasionally until clams open.

3. Meanwhile, cook linguine in a large, deep pot in rapidly boiling salted water until al dente. Drain linguine.

4. When all the clams are open, uncover the saucepan and add chopped fresh clams, or canned chopped clams (if using), oregano, and parsley. Cook 1 minute, to heat through.

5. Return drained linguine to large pot over medium-high heat, and stir in the clam sauce. Using a wooden spoon, toss together for 1 minute. Remove from heat and serve immediately.

Note: If pink clam sauce (marechiare) is desired, add tomatoes during step 2 when the clams are added.

LINGUINE WITH GARLIC AND OIL

Linguine Aglio e Olio

SERVES 4 AS A MAIN COURSE • SERVES 6 AS AN APPETIZER

1 pound linguine

1 cup Flavored Olive Oil (see page 10)

3 large garlic cloves, peeled and minced

Pinch dried red-pepper flakes, optional

Salt to taste

1 tablespoon chopped Italian parsley

1. Cook linguine in a large, deep pot in rapidly boiling salted water until al dente.

2. While linguine is cooking, heat oil in a medium sauté pan over medium heat. Add the garlic and, if using, red-pepper flakes and sauté for about 3 minutes or until garlic is golden. Add salt. Do not allow garlic to get too dark or it may turn bitter. Remove from heat and keep warm.

3. Drain linguine, reserving ½ cup of the cooking liquid. Return drained linguine and reserved cooking water to the pot. Place over medium-high heat and stir in the warm oil-and-garlic mixture. Using a wooden spoon, toss together for 1 minute. Remove from heat and serve, sprinkled with parsley.

Note: You can also season with freshly ground black pepper, but do not use both red and black or pasta will be too pungently flavored.

You may also flavor the sauce with 6 finely chopped anchovies packed in oil. Stir the chopped anchovies into the oil and garlic for the final 1 minute of sautéing. Proceed as above.

Did I ever tell you about the time, during the Gulf War, Kim and I were having dinner and the French ambassador was there with security guards everywhere? He even had a van parked outside, also filled with security. We had called a car that night. As we were leaving, I guess they thought I was the ambassador, because this stretch limo pulled up. Obviously not the type of car I was used to—with the dice hanging from the rearview mirror. I thought, "Wow! They're really getting classy around here." I thought it was ours, so Kim and I started to get into the limo and all these guys with guns jumped out, wondering what we were doing in the ambassador's car. Of course they were very polite about the situation. They thought we were trying to steal the ambassador's car!

Rao's is like my home away from home. Your cooking reminds me of my mother's and my grandmother's before her. When I feel like a home-cooked meal, Rao's is the place to go. And being the frustrated singer I am it gives me a place to be on stage. I am still hoping somebody up there will sign me!

JOEY HUNTER

SPAGHETTINI WITH BROCCOLI

Spaghettini con Broccoli

SERVES 4 AS A MAIN COURSE • SERVES 6 AS AN APPETIZER

---

1 pound spaghettini

1 cup Flavored Olive Oil (see page 10)

3 garlic cloves, peeled and minced

1 pound broccoli, cooked (see page 141)

½ cup Chicken Broth (see page 8)

Salt and pepper to taste

Freshly grated Pecorino Romano cheese

1. Cook spaghettini in a large, deep pot in rapidly boiling salted water until al dente.

2. While spaghettini is cooking, heat oil in a large sauté pan over medium-high heat. Sauté the garlic. Add cooked broccoli, Chicken Broth, salt and pepper, and simmer for 4 to 5 minutes. Set aside.

3. Drain spaghettini. Return drained spaghettini to the pot. Place over medium-high heat and stir in the broccoli mixture. Using a wooden spoon, toss together for 1 minute. Taste and adjust seasoning with salt and pepper. Remove from heat and serve, sprinkled with Pecorino Romano cheese.

Note: Broccoli may be replaced with 1 pound of cooked Savoy cabbage (see page 140), 1 pound of cooked broccoli rabe (see page 138), or 1 pound of cooked escarole (see page 140).

A trip to N.Y. isn't complete without a visit to Rao's, so any cookbook that gives recipes from this terrific family-run business is something I would keep in my kitchen at all times.

FRAN DRESCHER

Orecchiette with Broccoli Rabe and Sausage

Orecchiette con Broccoli di Rape e Salsiccia

Orecchiette, "little ears" in Italian, are small disc- or ear-shaped semolina pastas once made only at home. If you can't find this shape, any ridged or tubular small pasta will hold this sauce just fine.

The bitter rabe is nicely balanced by the intensity of the hot and sweet sausage to produce a very appetizing combination of flavors.

SERVES 4 AS A MAIN COURSE · SERVES 6 AS A PASTA COURSE

¼ cup Flavored Olive Oil (see page 10)

4 garlic cloves, peeled and chopped

1 pound Italian sausage, a combination of hot and sweet according to your taste, cut into bite-size pieces

1 pound broccoli rabe, cooked (see page 138)

1 cup broccoli rabe water (see page 138)

Salt and pepper to taste

1 pound orecchiette

Freshly-grated Pecorino Romano cheese

1. Heat oil and stir in garlic in a large sauté pan over medium heat. Add the sausages and sauté until meat is cooked and loses its raw look.

2. Add cooked broccoli rabe to sausage. Add rabe water, and salt and pepper to taste.

3. Raise heat and cook until sauce is hot.

4. Meanwhile, cook orecchiette in rapidly boiling salted water until al dente.

5. Drain orecchiette. Return drained orecchiette to the pot. Place over medium-high heat and stir in ¾ cup of broccoli rabe and sausage sauce. Using a wooden spoon, toss together for 1 minute. Remove from heat and pour into a large serving platter or bowl. Spoon remaining sauce over the top. Sprinkle with Pecorino Romano cheese.

I've eaten in restaurants all over the world, and Rao's undeniably puts them all to shame!

MARIAH CAREY

Penne with Cabbage, Sausage, and Marinara Sauce

SERVES 4 AS A MAIN COURSE · SERVES 6 AS A PASTA COURSE

¼ cup olive oil

4 cloves garlic, peeled and mashed

1 pound Italian sausage, cut into bite-size pieces

1 pound savoy cabbage, cooked (see page 140), chopped into bite-size pieces

Salt and pepper to taste

3 cups Marinara Sauce (see page 5)

1 pound penne

Freshly grated Pecorino Romano cheese, optional

1. Heat oil and garlic in a large sauté pan over medium heat. Add sausage, and sauté until meat is cooked.

2. Add cabbage, and salt and pepper to taste, and sauté for an additional 1–2 minutes. Stir in marinara sauce, and cook for 3–5 minutes, until flavors have blended.

3. Meanwhile, cook penne in a large, deep pot in rapidly boiling salted water until al dente.

4. Drain pasta, and return it to the pot with ½ cup of sauce. Stir for one minute over high heat, then place sauced pasta on serving platter and pour remaining sauce on top. Serve with a sprinkle of Pecorino Romano cheese, if desired.

Born and raised on East 109th Street, I grew up savoring the sights, sounds, and tastes of Rao's neighborhood. Being taken to the restaurant for the first time with older cousins felt like a rite of passage, a movement into an exclusive group of culinary cognoscenti. The food at Rao's unfailingly recalls for me the sumptuous Neapolitan fare I enjoyed at home, while Frank's unique style of hospitality makes me feel I am at home! Here's to the next hundred years at Rao's!

MICHAEL ROMANO

Rigatoni all'Arrabbiata

SERVES 4 AS A MAIN COURSE · SERVES 6 AS A PASTA COURSE

½ cup fine-quality olive oil

5 garlic cloves, peeled and minced

6 cups hand-crushed, canned, imported San Marzano Italian plum tomatoes, with juice

Salt to taste

2 teaspoons red-pepper flakes, or more, according to taste

Pinch dried oregano

6 to 8 fresh basil leaves, torn

1 pound rigatoni

¼ cup freshly grated Pecorino Romano cheese

1. Heat oil in a large saucepan over medium heat. Add garlic and sauté for about 4 minutes or until garlic is golden.

2. Stir in the tomatoes. Add salt. Bring to a boil. Lower heat and stir in red pepper flakes and simmer for about 20 minutes or until sauce has thickened slightly. Add a pinch of oregano and stir in basil just before ready to use.

3. Meanwhile, cook rigatoni in a large, deep pot in rapidly boiling salted water until al dente.

4. Drain rigatoni, reserving ½ cup cooking water. Return drained rigatoni and reserved water to the pot. Place over medium-high heat and stir in 1 to 2 cups sauce and the cheese. Using a wooden spoon, toss together for 1 minute. Remove from heat and serve.

After years of attending weddings at the Pierre and the Plaza, when it came time for mine, when I had to pick my favorite place in the world—it was Rao's, of course.

After a midtown ceremony, we piled into limousines and wended our way uptown to 114th Street. As someone who spends more time on Park and Madison than the IRT, the trip up First Avenue always holds an air of mystery and journey to unfamiliar and exciting terrain. Then Rao's opens its doors and its heart. I did the tables in a formal style and, as I still owned The Green Thumb, created cascaded arrangements, and Rao's rolled a red carpet into the street.

Annie Rao did all the cooking, and I didn't invite my mother. I guess that tells you whom I consider family.

SUSAN KASEN SUMMER

Spaghetti alla Carbonara

SERVES 4 AS A MAIN COURSE • SERVES 6 AS A PASTA COURSE

¼ cup olive oil

1 tablespoon unsalted butter

1 medium yellow onion, peeled and minced

4 ounces pancetta (or prosciutto), diced

3 large egg yolks, room temperature

½ cup heavy cream, room temperature

½ cup grated Parmigiano Reggiano cheese,
   room temperature

1 pound spaghetti

Freshly ground black pepper to taste

1. Heat oil and butter in a large sauté pan over medium heat. Add onion and pancetta, and cook until the pancetta is slightly crisp. Remove from heat and set aside.

2. In a bowl, whisk the egg yolks, cream, and cheese.

3. In a large pot of rapidly boiling salted water, cook the pasta until al dente. Drain and return to the pot.

4. Add the cooked onion and pancetta to the pot, and stir over high heat until the pasta is coated.

5. Remove the pasta from the heat, and add the egg, cheese, and cream mixture. Toss until pasta is coated. Season with freshly ground pepper, and serve immediately.

It's real simple: There is only one real Italian restaurant in America . . . It's Rao's!

Every dish reminds me of being back home, when my mother and grandmother were the two greatest chefs in my life.

The Old World saloon atmosphere is fun for everyone to enjoy. And, of course, it's always my favorite time of year at Rao's: Christmas!

THOMAS D. MOTTOLA

LASAGNE

½ cup plus 2 tablespoons fine-quality olive oil

1 cup chopped onion

1 tablespoon minced garlic

2 pounds lean ground beef

1 pound hot or sweet Italian sausage meat, removed from casings and chopped

½ cup red wine

3 28-ounce cans imported San Marzano Italian tomatoes, with juice, hand-crushed

3 tablespoons tomato paste

5 cups water

Salt and pepper to taste

2 pounds ricotta cheese

2 egg yolks

1 pound lasagne noodles

2 cups grated fresh mozzarella cheese

1 cup freshly grated Pecorino Romano cheese

1 pound fresh mozzarella cheese, sliced

1. Heat ½ cup oil in a large saucepan over medium-high heat. Add onion and garlic and sauté for 3 minutes. Stir in the beef and sauté for 5 minutes or until well browned. Remove the beef with a slotted spoon and set aside. Add the sausage to the saucepan and sauté until browned. Return beef to saucepan.

2. Add the wine to the saucepan and cook for 5 minutes or until it has evaporated.

3. Stir in tomatoes, tomato paste, and water. Add salt and pepper. Simmer, stirring occasionally, for about 2 hours or until thick and rich in flavor. If needed, add more water, a quarter cup at a time. If sauce is fatty, either skim off the fat or put a few layers of paper towel on the top to absorb the excess fat. (If you have the time, refrigerate the sauce until the fat congeals on top; then simply lift it off.)

4. Put ricotta into a cheesecloth-lined colander and allow it to drain in the refrigerator for about 2 hours. Combine with egg yolks; blend well. This will keep the lasagne from being watery.

5. Add the noodles and remaining 2 tablespoons oil to a large, deep pot filled with rapidly boiling salted water. Cook noodles until al dente. Drain well in a colander and then run under cold running water to stop the cooking process. Put noodles, in a single layer, on clean, damp kitchen towels. Cover with clean, damp towels.

6. Preheat oven to 350∞ F.

7. Ladle a thin layer of meat sauce into a lasagne pan (12 ¥ 18 ¥ 2 inches or 14 ¥ 10 ¥ 3 inches). Cover with noodles, laid lengthwise, then cover noodles with a layer of meat sauce. Spread a thin, smooth layer of ricotta over the meat sauce. Sprinkle with grated mozzarella and Pecorino Romano. Continue layers of pasta, sauce, and cheese, alternating the pasta in opposite directions for each layer (lengthwise, then crosswise, etc.). Finish with a layer of meat sauce covered with sliced mozzarella and sprinkle with Pecorino Romano.

8. Bake in preheated oven for about 45 minutes or until cheese topping has melted and lasagne is bubbling.

9. Remove from oven and allow to rest for 15 minutes before cutting into squares and serving.

Note: Lasagne noodles can be replaced with the pasta crepes used to make Manicotti (see page 55). Make 9- to 10-inch crepes and cut them into 2½-inch-wide strips.

Manicotti

2 large eggs

2 cups whole milk

1½ cups all-purpose flour

Approximately 2 tablespoons vegetable oil

2 cups ricotta cheese

2 large egg yolks

1 cup finely diced fresh mozzarella cheese

½ cup freshly grated Pecorino Romano cheese

Salt and freshly ground white pepper to taste

4 cups Marinara Sauce (see page 5)

12 ¼-inch-thick slices mozzarella cheese, approximately 3 inches long by 1 inch wide

1. In a medium bowl, whisk together the eggs and milk. When well combined, whisk in flour until smooth. Set aside to rest for about 1 hour.

2. Heat a nonstick crepe pan over medium-high heat. Lightly brush it with vegetable oil and return to heat. Pour a little less than ½ cup of batter into the pan, swirling to cover the bottom evenly. Cook for about 30 seconds or until it is just set and the bottom is lightly browned. Turn the crepe over carefully with a spatula or a fork. Cook for an additional 15 seconds or until set. Remove from pan and place on a piece of waxed paper. Continue cooking and stacking crepes until you have at least 14. The extra 2 will allow for breakage.

3. Using a wooden spoon, combine ricotta, egg yolks, diced mozzarella, Pecorino Romano cheese, and salt and pepper until well blended.

4. Preheat oven to 375° F.

5. Lay crepes out in a single layer. Place a heaping tablespoonful of the ricotta mixture in the center at the top of the crepe, spreading out to the edges. Fold the ricotta-covered portion over onto the crepe. Fold the edges in and roll into a firm packet.

6. Spread Marinara Sauce over the bottom of a 13 × 9 × 2-inch baking pan. Lay rolled crepes on top of the Marinara Sauce. Put a slice of mozzarella on top of each rolled crepe.

7. Bake manicotti in preheated oven for about 12 minutes or until filling is hot and cheese has melted. Serve, allowing 2 pieces per person.

Pasta Filetto di Pomodoro

SERVES 4 AS A MAIN COURSE · SERVES 6 AS A PASTA COURSE

⅓ cup fine-quality olive oil

2 to 4 ounces chopped pancetta or
   prosciutto

¾ cup chopped onion

6 cups hand-crushed, canned, imported San
   Marzano Italian plum tomatoes

Salt to taste

1 pound fusilli

6 to 8 leaves fresh basil, shredded

Pinch dried oregano

Black pepper to taste

2 tablespoons chopped Italian parsley

1. Heat oil in a large sauté pan over medium-high heat. Add pancetta and onions and sauté for about 5 minutes or until pancetta is slightly crisp and onions are beginning to brown.

2. Stir in tomatoes and bring to a boil. Lower heat and simmer for 30 minutes or until flavors are well blended. Add salt.

3. When ready to serve, cook the fusilli in rapidly boiling salted water until al dente.

4. About 2 minutes before serving, stir fresh basil, oregano, and pepper into the sauce.

5. Drain fusilli. Return drained fusilli to the pot. Place over medium-high heat and stir in ½ cup sauce. Using a wooden spoon, toss together for 1 minute. Remove from heat and pour into a large serving platter or bowl. Spoon remaining sauce over the top. Sprinkle parsley over all and serve.

When you mention Rao's to someone, you can see their eyes light up. Probably they've never been there—you can't get in the place—but they've heard about it: the location, the ambience, the mystique, all those stories. You can only imagine what it is like. And then one night, you get lucky. You get in and find out it's all true.

REGIS PHILBIN

Pappardelle with Hot Sausage Sauce

The wide, rich pappardelle noodle is perfect to catch this savory, slightly spicy sauce. If you don't like a spicy sauce, substitute sweet sausage for the hot for an equally delicious accompaniment.

SERVES 4 AS A MAIN COURSE · SERVES 6 AS A PASTA COURSE

6 hot or sweet Italian sausages

¼ cup fine-quality olive oil

¾ cup chopped onion

1½ cups dry white wine

2 28-ounce cans imported San Marzano Italian plum tomatoes, hand-crushed

Salt to taste

6 fresh basil leaves, torn

Pinch dried oregano

Freshly ground black pepper to taste

1 pound pappardelle noodles

2 tablespoons freshly grated Pecorino Romano cheese, plus more to taste, if desired

1. Remove casing from sausages and break meat up into chunks. Set aside.

2. Heat oil in a large sauté pan over medium-high heat. Add onions and sauté for 3 minutes or until just translucent. Stir in sausage meat and sauté for about 5 minutes or until lightly browned.

3. Drain off excess fat. Add wine and stir to combine. Raise heat and bring to a boil. Boil for about 3 minutes or until liquid has reduced slightly.

4. Add tomatoes and salt. Return to a boil, then lower heat and simmer for about 20 minutes or until sauce has thickened slightly. Stir in basil, oregano, and pepper. Taste and, if necessary, adjust seasoning with salt and pepper.

5. While sauce is simmering, cook the pappardelle in a large, deep pot in rapidly boiling salted water until al dente.

6. Drain pappardelle. Return drained pappardelle to the pot. Over medium-high heat, stir in ½ cup sausage sauce. Using a wooden spoon, toss together for 1 minute. Remove from heat and pour into a large serving platter or bowl. Spoon remaining sauce over the top. Sprinkle with 2 tablespoons of Pecorino Romano cheese. Pass additional cheese, if desired.

SHELLS WITH RICOTTA

SERVES 4 AS A MAIN COURSE · SERVES 6 AS A PASTA COURSE

1 pound large pasta shells

2 cups fresh ricotta cheese

6 cups Marinara Sauce (see page 5)

¼ cup freshly grated Pecorino Romano cheese

Salt and pepper to taste

2 tablespoons chopped Italian parsley

1. Cook the shells in a large, deep pot in rapidly boiling salted water until al dente.

2. Meanwhile, combine ricotta, 4 cups Marinara Sauce, and Pecorino Romano cheese in a medium saucepan over medium-low heat. Cook, stirring constantly, for 4 minutes or until well combined and hot. Adjust seasoning with salt and pepper. Remove from heat. Cover and keep warm.

3. Warm remaining Marinara Sauce in a small saucepan over low heat.

4. Drain shells. Return drained shells to the pot. Over medium-high heat, stir in ½ cup ricotta sauce. Using a wooden spoon, toss together for 1 minute. Remove from heat and stir in remaining ricotta sauce. Spoon onto a large serving platter with a ladleful of Marinara Sauce over the top. Sprinkle with parsley and serve.

Rao's has to take the praise (or blame) for my latest novel, Pretend You Don't See Her.

I was having dinner there last June. My publishers had been after me to divulge the plot and title of my next book. They absolutely needed that information for the catalog.

I just wasn't settled on either. Several ideas were bouncing around in my mind. I often try to find a song title that works with the story line when I begin a new effort. But nothing was jelling.

Then that lovely June evening as I was happily enjoying the fabulous food at Rao's, Frank Pellegrino, the owner who is both a singer and an actor, picked up a mike and began to sing an old Jerry Vale song, "Pretend You Don't See Her."

One of the ideas I'd been kicking around was about a young woman who witnesses a murder and is forced to hide in the Federal Witness Protection Program.

That's my story, *I thought, because* that's my title.

A thousand thanks, Frank. Now, how about singing another song next time I'm at Rao's? It's catalog time again!

MARY HIGGINS CLARK

Spaghetti alla Puttanesca

SERVES 4 AS A MAIN COURSE · SERVES 6 AS A PASTA COURSE

¾ cup fine-quality olive oil

1 cup finely diced onion

3 garlic cloves, peeled and minced

6 anchovy fillets, chopped

¼ cup dry white wine

4 cups hand-crushed, canned, imported San Marzano Italian plum tomatoes, with juice

1 cup Gaeta (or other brine-cured black olives) olives, pitted and sliced

2 tablespoons salt-packed capers, well rinsed

Dried red-pepper flakes to taste, optional

Salt and pepper to taste

1 pound spaghetti

10 fresh basil leaves, torn

Pinch dried oregano

2 tablespoons chopped Italian parsley

1. Place oil, onion, and garlic in a large sauté pan over medium-low heat. Sauté for about 5 minutes or until onions are translucent but not brown. Stir in anchovies and sauté until anchovies have dissolved into the oil.

2. Raise heat and add wine. Bring to a boil, then stir in tomatoes, olives, capers, and, if using, red-pepper flakes. Return to a boil. Lower heat and simmer for 5 minutes. Taste and adjust seasoning with salt and pepper and simmer for 10 minutes.

3. Meanwhile, cook spaghetti in a large, deep pot in rapidly boiling salted water until al dente.

4. Just before serving, stir basil and oregano into the sauce.

5. Drain spaghetti. Return drained spaghetti to the pot. Over medium-high heat, stir in ½ cup sauce. Using a wooden spoon, toss together for 1 minute. Remove from heat and pour into a large serving platter or bowl. Spoon remaining sauce over the top. Sprinkle with parsley and serve.

Back in 1970, when I first walked into Rao's, it was like walking into history . . . like walking into the 1920s, like walking into the 1930s, like walking into the 1940s, like walking into the 1950s—all combined. It seems that problems go away there. You meet the friendliest people. Even if they are not friendly, they sure act friendly.

The warmth of Rao's, the feeling of being with my family—Frankie, Frankie junior, Nicky, and Ron—makes all my troubles go away. I am very fortunate to have had my table every Thursday night since 1977 . . . but I am also at Rao's at least three times a week.

Rao's, with the best food in the world and the best music in the world, makes you want to get up and sing even if your voice is not so good . . . it does not matter.

The best time of the year to be at Rao's is around Christmas. The holiday season becomes even more spirited with the warm feeling you have there. Every Christmas Eve before I go home to my family, it has become my tradition to spend an early evening in Rao's. I reflect upon the whole year that has just passed. I am in a very happy yet melancholy mood. As 10:00 P.M. approaches I leave, but I will be back next week—to my Rao's.

RICHARD "BO" DIETL

Fusilli with Fresh Tomatoes and Mozzarella

SERVES 4 AS A MAIN COURSE · SERVES 6 AS A PASTA COURSE

½ cup fine-quality olive oil

3 garlic cloves, peeled and minced

3 pounds very ripe plum tomatoes, peeled, cored, seeded, and diced

½ cup torn fresh basil leaves, loosely packed

Salt and freshly ground white pepper to taste

1 pound fusilli

2 cups diced fresh mozzarella cheese

1. Heat oil and garlic in a large sauté pan over very low heat. Add the tomatoes, half of the basil, and salt and pepper and remove from heat. Cover and let rest for at least 15 minutes.

2. While sauce is resting, cook fusilli in a large, deep pot in rapidly boiling salted water until al dente.

3. Drain fusilli. Return drained fusilli to the pot. Stir in the tomato sauce. Using a wooden spoon, toss together for 1 minute. Spoon onto a large serving platter and top with mozzarella. Garnish with remaining basil, and serve.

I have been going to Rao's for over thirty-five years, I guess. At least it seems that way . . . If they were open that long ago. The blessed Nick the Vest happened to serve me my first legal drink at eighteen. I do happen to have a story about Rao's.

I think the most interesting story—besides singing doo-wop with Joey Hunter, you know, those Shirelles and Frankie Lymon tunes on the greatest jukebox in New York City—was one time I had just come back from Los Angeles. While I was driving in my car I suddenly remembered that I had sent some important clients to Rao's for dinner that night. I wanted to stop by and say hello. So I went to Rao's, parked my car in front of the restaurant, and ran in.

I said hello to my clients, had a glass of wine . . . before you knew it, I was sitting down and eating some chicken and sausage dish, then some ziti with broccoli rabe . . . I was having a fabulous time! Finally, I realized that time had flown and I had to leave. I went out to my car parked in front of the restaurant. I went up to the car. I looked at it, it was my car, but . . . the keys were in the ignition, and the engine was running! Where else in East Harlem but on 114th Street in front of Rao's could I leave my car with the motor running, have dinner, and still find it there when I left?

I have always had a fondness for the whole Rao's family.

PHIL SUAREZ

Sunday Gravy

MAKES 3 QUARTS

1-pound piece lean beef, such as eye of round

1-pound piece lean pork, such as loin

1 pound hot or sweet Italian sausages

½ cup fine-quality olive oil

4 garlic cloves, peeled

3 tablespoons tomato paste

¼ cup water

3 35-ounce cans imported San Marzano Italian plum tomatoes, hand-crushed, reserving the juice

Salt and pepper to taste

1 recipe Beef Braciola (see page 110)

1 recipe Anna and Frankie's Meatballs (see page 106), optional

1. With a paper towel, pat the meat dry.

2. Heat oil in a large saucepan or deep, heavy-bottomed casserole over medium heat. Add garlic and toss to coat.

3. Cook meat, a few pieces at a time, in the oil for about 5 minutes, turning frequently, until nicely browned on all sides. As meat is browned, remove from pan and set aside. When garlic cloves begin to brown, remove and discard them.

4. Combine tomato paste and water and stir into the oil. Cook, stirring constantly, for 2 to 3 minutes. Stir in the tomatoes and the juice, raise heat, and bring to a boil. Using one of the tomato cans, measure 2 cans of cold water and add to the pan. Return to a boil.

5. Return beef and pork to the sauce and add salt and pepper. Bring to a boil and allow to boil for 5 minutes.

6. Lower heat and partially cover the pan. Simmer, stirring occasionally, for about 2 hours or until meat is almost falling apart and sauce is thick. If sauce becomes too thick, add water, a quarter cup at a time.

7. One hour before sauce is ready, add Beef Braciola and sausage.

8. If using, add the Meatballs at the same time.

9. Remove meat from the sauce. Serve sauce over pasta, then meat as a separate course.

Note: The more meat, the richer and thicker the sauce. You can add any type of beef, pork, or veal that you prefer or you can use only one type of meat. Rolled beef, called braciola, is one of the traditional meats used and many Italian cooks feel that the sausage is absolutely necessary for great flavor.

POTATO GNOCCHI

MAKES ABOUT 80 PIECES

4 pounds baking potatoes

Salt to taste

2 large eggs

3 tablespoons unsalted butter, melted

3 cups all-purpose flour

2 teaspoons fine-quality olive oil

Veal Sauce for Gnocchi (see page 70)

1. Put the whole potatoes in a large saucepan with cold water to cover. Add salt and bring to a boil over high heat. Lower heat and simmer for about 30 minutes or until the potatoes are cooked. Drain and set aside until cool enough to handle.

2. Peel, quarter, and mash the potatoes until they are smooth. Beat in the eggs and butter. When well blended, slowly add 2 cups of flour, sifting in a small amount at a time, beating well after each addition. The amount of flour will vary depending upon the moisture in the potatoes. You should add sufficient flour to make a dough that is smooth and elastic enough to form into gnocchi easily.

3. Place remaining 1 cup flour in a small bowl.

4. Turn the dough out onto a lightly floured surface and roll it out by hand to about a ½-inch thickness. Cut into pieces about 1 inch long and about ½ inch wide.

5. Using the flour in the bowl, dust your hands and toss the gnocchi in your hands to lightly coat each piece with flour. Gently press the top of your index finger into the center of each piece to make a slight indentation. Let gnocchi rest for 30 minutes.

6. Bring a large pot of salted water to a boil. Add oil and then gnocchi. Boil for about 5 minutes or until gnocchi rise to the top. Using a slotted spoon, lift the gnocchi from the water as they rise. Drain well. Spoon onto a warm serving platter and pour Veal Sauce over the top.

Note: Gnocchi can be frozen after the resting period. Lay out, in one layer, on a cookie sheet and freeze for 4 hours; then place in a resealable plastic bag, label and date, and freeze for up to 6 months. To cook, follow above directions but allow additional cooking time.

Gnocchi alla Romana

Gnocchi, although not pasta, are a perfect first course. These semolina dumplings, prepared in the Roman style, are light as air and ready to embrace any sauce you choose. At Rao's, we usually prepare 6 pieces per person—each topped with mozzarella cheese, which is then melted under the broiler—served on a pool of steaming Marinara Sauce.

MAKES ABOUT 60 PIECES

8 cups whole milk

2 pounds semolina flour

8 tablespoons salted butter, cubed

1 tablespoon salt

1 teaspoon black pepper

5 egg yolks

1. Warm milk in a large, heavy saucepan over medium heat. Whisk in flour, butter, salt, and pepper, and bring to a simmer, stirring constantly.

2. Lower heat and cook, stirring constantly with a long-handled wooden spoon, for 30 minutes or until batter pulls away from the side of the pan in a solid mass. (You must constantly bring the batter up and away from the sides and bottom of the pan or it will stick.) At the last minute, add the egg yolks, mix in, and cook for 2 to 3 minutes.

3. Remove from heat and pour the batter onto a nonstick cookie sheet with sides, spreading it out with a spatula to form a rectangle of even thickness. To prevent it from sticking, you may have to dip the spatula in cold water from time to time so that it glides over the top. Cover lightly and set aside to cool.

4. When cool, cut into circles using a small (1½-inch round) cookie or biscuit cutter.

5. At this point, you can either put the circles on a well-buttered sheet pan, dot with butter, sprinkle with freshly grated cheese, and bake in a preheated 400° F oven for 15 minutes or until golden, or serve them as we do at Rao's, topped with a circle of mozzarella, broiled for about 2 to 3 minutes or until cheese is golden, and served in a pool of Marinara Sauce.

Note: Gnocchi can be made up to 2 days in advance. Store, tightly covered and refrigerated.

Veal Sauce for Gnocchi

MAKES ABOUT 2 QUARTS

1 cup fine-quality olive oil

2½ pounds veal stew meat, cut into bite-size
pieces

¼ cup finely diced prosciutto

1½ cups chopped white mushrooms

1 cup diced onion

½ cup grated carrot

¼ cup finely diced celery

2 teaspoons minced garlic

1 tablespoon all-purpose flour

3 cups Chicken Broth (see page 8)

1½ cups dry white wine

4 cups hand-crushed, canned, imported San
Marzano Italian plum tomatoes, with juice

Salt and pepper to taste

1. Heat ½ cup oil in a large, heavy saucepan over medium-high heat. Add the veal and cook, stirring frequently, for about 10 minutes or until meat has begun to brown. Stir in ham and sauté for an additional 5 minutes.

2. While veal is browning, place remaining oil in a medium sauté pan over medium heat. Sauté the mushrooms for 5 minutes or until most of the juices have cooked out and the mushrooms are lightly browned. Strain and set aside.

3. Stir onion into veal and sauté for 3 minutes. Stir in carrot, celery, and garlic and sauté for 2 minutes. Add the drained mushrooms and sauté for an additional 1 minute. Spoon off excess oil.

4. Sprinkle flour over the meat mixture and cook, stirring constantly, for 3 minutes or until flour is well incorporated.

5. Pour in broth and wine. Raise heat and, stirring frequently, bring to a boil. Lower heat and simmer for 10 minutes.

6. Stir in tomatoes and salt and pepper. Bring to a boil. Lower heat and simmer, stirring occasionally, for 2 hours or until meat is very tender and sauce is quite thick. Serve as a sauce for gnocchi, a flavoring for risotto, or as a gravy on any broad noodle (such as pappardelle) or ridged pasta (such as rigatoni or fusilli).

Note: Veal Sauce will keep, tightly covered and refrigerated, for up to 3 days or frozen for up to 3 months. Thaw and reheat for at least 15 minutes before using.

RISOTTO

Risotto Milanese

SERVES 6 AS A MAIN COURSE

Approximately 6 cups Chicken or Meat Broth (see pages 8 and 7)

¼ teaspoon saffron threads

3 tablespoons unsalted butter

3 tablespoons fine-quality olive oil

3 tablespoons finely minced onion

2 cups Arborio (or other Italian short-grained) rice

½ cup freshly grated Pecorino Romano cheese

Salt to taste

1. Warm broth in a large saucepan over low heat.

2. Remove ¼ cup broth and crush saffron threads into it. Allow saffron to soak for at least 15 minutes.

3. Heat butter and oil in a heavy-bottomed, 6-quart saucepan over medium heat. Add the onion and sauté for about 5 minutes or until onion is very soft and just beginning to turn golden.

4. Add the rice and sauté for about 2 minutes or until it is glistening and the grains are well coated.

5. Stirring constantly, add hot broth, ½ cup at a time, adding additional broth as liquid is absorbed. When you have added 3½ cups of broth, pour the saffron-flavored broth through a fine sieve into the rice, stirring constantly. When this is absorbed, taste for tenderness. If rice is still hard, continue adding broth, stirring constantly, until rice has absorbed enough liquid to be al dente with a creamy consistency.

6. Remove from heat and stir in ¼ cup cheese. When well blended, taste and adjust seasoning.

7. Serve in shallow soup bowls, sprinkled with the remaining cheese.

Aside from the great food (and what a neighborhood), I'll never forget the time I sang my copyrighted birthday ditty to Bo Dietl! What a time. I only hope this gets me a table.

TONY DANZA

Risotto with Fresh Asparagus

Risotto con Asparagi

SERVES 6

1 pound fresh asparagus

Salt to taste

Approximately 4 cups Chicken or Meat Broth
  (see pages 8 and 7)

2 tablespoons unsalted butter

2 tablespoons fine-quality olive oil

3 tablespoons finely minced onion

2 cups Arborio (or other Italian short-
  grained) rice

¼ cup freshly grated Pecorino Romano
  cheese

Freshly ground black pepper to taste

1. Trim the tough ends from the asparagus. Peel off the tough skin from around the bottom of the stalk. Put the cleaned asparagus into a pan that can hold it lying flat. Add cold water to cover by 1 inch and salt. Bring to a boil over medium-high heat. Cover, lower heat, and simmer for 4 minutes or until asparagus is just tender but still firm. Drain the asparagus, reserving cooking water. Set asparagus aside to cool.

2. Cut the cooled asparagus into 1½-inch pieces, reserving the tips separately. Set aside.

3. Combine the asparagus cooking water with enough broth to make 6 cups liquid. Place in a medium saucepan over low heat.

4. Heat butter and oil in a heavy-bottomed, 6-quart saucepan over medium heat. Add the onion and sauté for about 5 minutes or until onion is very soft and just beginning to turn golden.

5. Add the rice and sauté for about 2 minutes or until it is glistening. Stir in the asparagus pieces and immediately begin adding hot broth mixture, ½ cup at a time, stirring constantly, adding additional broth as liquid is absorbed. When rice has absorbed enough liquid to be al dente and of a creamy consistency, remove from heat and stir in the reserved asparagus tips, cheese, and pepper. Taste and, if necessary, add salt. Serve immediately.

A triple-A restaurant, run by a true "blue chip" guy.

DICK GRASSO

CO-OWNERS RON STRACI AND FRANK PELLEGRINO

RISOTTO WITH SHELLFISH

Risotto con Frutti di Mare

SERVES 6

7 tablespoons fine-quality olive oil

½ pound squid, cleaned and cut into rings

¾ cup dry white wine

1 pound small cherrystone clams, well scrubbed

½ pound bay scallops

½ pound small shrimp, peeled and deveined, with tails removed

1 cup bottled clam juice

2 tablespoons unsalted butter

2 cups Arborio (or other Italian short-grained) rice

Approximately 4 cups water

3 tablespoons chopped Italian parsley

Salt to taste

1. Heat 2 tablespoons oil in a heavy sauté pan over medium heat. Add the squid and sauté for 3 minutes. Add ½ cup wine and cook for about 20 minutes or until squid is tender and all liquid has evaporated. Remove from heat and set aside.

2. Heat 2 tablespoons oil in a large saucepan over medium-high heat. Add the clams and cook, covered, for about 5-10 minutes or until all clams have opened. Remove from heat and separate the clams from their shells, reserving any liquid and discarding the shells. Add the clams to the squid along with any reserved liquid. Stir the scallops and shrimp into the squid and clams and place over medium heat. Cook for 2 minutes. Remove from heat and set aside.

3. Warm clam juice in a small saucepan over low heat.

4. Heat remaining oil and the butter in a heavy-bottomed, 6-quart saucepan over medium heat. Add the rice and sauté for 2 minutes or until rice is glistening. Add the remaining wine and cook, stirring constantly, until wine is absorbed.

5. Add the hot clam juice to the rice, stirring constantly. When clam juice has been absorbed, begin adding hot water, ½ cup at a time, stirring constantly, adding additional water as liquid is absorbed.

6. When rice is al dente and has a creamy consistency, remove from heat and immediately stir in reserved shellfish and parsley. Taste and, if necessary, adjust seasoning with salt. Serve immediately.

Risotto with Veal Sauce

SERVES 6

Approximately 5 cups Meat Broth (see
page 7)

1½ cups Veal Sauce for Gnocchi (see
page 70)

2 cups Arborio (or other Italian short-
grained) rice

¼ cup freshly grated Parmigiano-Reggiano
cheese

Salt to taste

1. Warm broth in a medium saucepan over low heat.

2. Put Veal Sauce in a heavy-bottomed, 6-quart saucepan over medium heat. When it begins
to simmer, stir in the rice and cook, stirring constantly, for 1 minute.

3. Stirring constantly, add the hot broth, ½ cup at a time, adding additional broth as liquid
is absorbed. Continue adding broth, stirring constantly, until rice has absorbed enough liquid
to be al dente and have a creamy consistency.

4. Remove from heat and stir in cheese. When well blended, taste and, if necessary, adjust
seasoning with salt. Serve immediately.

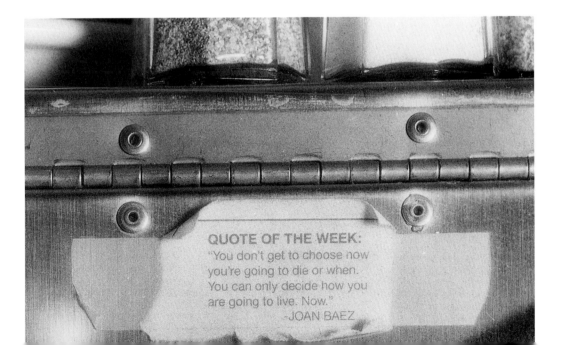

QUOTE OF THE WEEK:
"You don't get to choose how
you're going to die or when.
You can only decide how you
are going to live. Now."
-JOAN BAEZ

I remember the radio crackling. I could hear the announcer screaming that Rocky Graziano was the middleweight champion of the world. I was twelve years old and serving as an informal waiter during the Feast of Our Lady of Mount Carmel. It was July 1947.

During the feast, Rao's closed its kitchen so as not to compete with the sidewalk stands set up during the holiday. The young nephews, of whom I was one, were allowed to don the famous white aprons the uncles wore and help serve our customers. One slightly tipsy customer gave me a dollar bill and told me to play "Peg o' My Heart" twenty times on the jukebox. To be part of the mysteries of the "saloon" was an honor indeed.

Having spent every Sunday dinner I could remember with "Mama Jake," as my grandmother Francesca was called by her children and grandchildren, Rao's Bar and Grill, next door to my grandmother's, seemed like such a wonderful haven of good friends, fast smiles, and wonderful smells. My cousin Francesca Rao Tortorici remembers how in those days my great-uncle Joseph—Zi Pepe, as he was known to us—looked out for everyone in the neighborhood. Almost every night, recent immigrant families from La Polla would meet at Rao's. Zi Pepe would help them get jobs.

It made me proud to know that my uncles had the most famous restaurant in the neighborhood! Doctors, lawyers, ballplayers, entertainers, and scalawags were always in attendance. Francesca remembers that Rao's attracted immigrants from all over southern Italy, as well as underworld characters, especially during Prohibition. The very first celebrities to discover Rao's were Keenan Wynn, Frank Gifford, Gloria DeHaven, and Richard Burton. They were in Rao's every time they were in town.

And, of course, everyone looked up to my uncles who owned Rao's. Both were bachelors, and to a young man growing up they were two special men indeed. Although my uncle Vince married Anna Pellegrino late in life, he had dated her for so long that even Nathan Detroit and Miss Adelaide would have understood.

Uncle Lou reminded me of Clifton Webb. He dressed leisurely yet carefully each day. Sartorial splendor was a term that seemed to have been invented for him. Uncle Vince was more casual but nonetheless a polished dresser. I always remember his cars and his dogs. The cars, usually convertibles and mostly black Cadillacs, were always new; the dogs, usually large and black, were always secondhand. Strays found a home at Rao's.

Rao's has been many things for me. Only the passage of time has made me an owner, and if I could I would turn the clock back and watch my uncle Lou change the water in the cylinders on either side of the cash register that held goldfish, or ask my uncle Vince to show me his new car, I'd love to run through those years again. I enjoyed our time together and still savor the memories.

RON STRACI

Chicken

I guess one of my favorite memories about Rao's is the night Frankie stayed open late so I could celebrate my Broadway debut with family and friends. I've been lucky enough to dine there many times, and whether celebrating my girlfriend Lynn's birthday or just looking for a great meal, I don't think there's a better dining experience in New York. My personal favorites are the lemon chicken and the cheesecake . . . They're as good as it gets.

BRUNO KIRBY

Rao's Famous Lemon Chicken

Pollo al Limone

SERVES 6

---

2 2½- to 3-pound broiling chickens, halved   ¼ cup chopped Italian parsley

Lemon Sauce (recipe follows)

1. To attain maximum heat, preheat broiler for at least 15 minutes before using.

2. Broil chicken halves, turning once, for about 30 minutes or until skin is golden-brown and juices run clear when bird is pierced with a fork.

3. Remove chicken from broiler, leaving broiler on. Using a very sharp knife, cut each half into about 6 pieces (leg, thigh, wing, 3 small breast pieces).

4. Place chicken on a baking sheet with sides, of a size that can fit into the broiler. Pour Lemon Sauce over the chicken and toss to coat well. If necessary, divide sauce in half and do this in two batches.

5. Return to broiler and broil for 3 minutes. Turn each piece and broil for an additional minute.

6. Remove from broiler and portion each chicken onto each of 6 warm serving plates.

7. Pour sauce into a heavy saucepan. Stir in parsley and place over high heat for 1 minute. Pour an equal amount of sauce over each chicken and serve with lots of crusty bread to absorb the sauce.

LEMON SAUCE

---

2 cups fresh lemon juice   1½ teaspoons minced garlic

1 cup olive oil   ½ teaspoon dried oregano

1 tablespoon red wine vinegar   Salt and pepper to taste

1. Whisk together juice, oil, vinegar, garlic, oregano, and salt and pepper. Cover and refrigerate until ready to use. Whisk or shake vigorously before using.

ROAST CHICKEN WITH POTATOES

Pollo Arrosto con Patate

SERVES 6

---

6 to 8 medium all-purpose potatoes

1 5-pound roasting chicken

1 lemon

4 fresh rosemary sprigs or 3 teaspoons dried

Salt and pepper to taste

¼ cup fine-quality olive oil

1. Preheat oven to 450° F.

2. Peel potatoes and cut into quarters. Place in cold, salted water to cover and set aside.

3. Wash the chicken and pat dry. Cut the lemon in half and generously squeeze the juice into the cavity and on the skin, rubbing with the cut side as you squeeze.

4. Place 2 rosemary sprigs in the cavity along with the squeezed lemon halves. Using butcher's twine, tie the legs to the body.

5. Pull the leaves from the remaining rosemary sprigs and sprinkle them over the bird, tucking some into any skin openings.

6. Put the chicken on a rack in a roasting pan. Sprinkle with salt and pepper.

7. Drain the potatoes and pat them dry. Toss with olive oil and salt to taste. Scatter them around the chicken in the roasting pan.

8. Place chicken in preheated oven and roast, turning potatoes occasionally, for about 1½ hours or until chicken is golden-brown and juices run clear when meat is pierced with a knife and potatoes are crisp and nicely browned.

9. Remove from oven and let rest for 5 minutes before carving.

Rao's is the place we think of going to relax, see old friends, and sit back and hope that Frankie will sing some of his favorite songs!

LINDA BEAUCHAMP

CHICKEN CACCIATORA

Pollo alla Cacciatora

"Alla cacciatora" simply means "in the style of the hunter." Almost every household has its own version of this rich fricassee or stew, usually comprised of some type of poultry (or rabbit) with an assortment of vegetables cooked down to a rich sauce.

SERVES 6

2 2½- to 3-pound chickens

½ cup vegetable oil

2 green frying peppers, cored, seeded, and cut, lengthwise, into ½-inch-thick strips

1 medium red bell pepper, cored, seeded, and cut, lengthwise, into ½-inch-thick strips

1½ cups sliced white mushrooms

1 cup diced onion

1 cup dry white wine

2 cups Chicken Broth (see page 8)

4 cups hand-crushed, imported San Marzano Italian plum tomatoes

Salt and pepper to taste

½ teaspoon dried oregano

Pinch dried red-pepper flakes, optional

1. Cut chickens into small serving pieces (leg, thigh, wing, 2 to 3 breast pieces). Pat dry.

2. Heat oil in a large, deep casserole over medium-high heat. Add chicken and cook in batches, turning frequently, for about 10 minutes or until well browned.

3. Add peppers, mushrooms, and onion and sauté for about 5 minutes or until vegetables are soft but not brown. Drain off all excess oil.

4. Add wine and sauté for one minute.

5. Stir in broth, then tomatoes. Season with salt, pepper, oregano, and red pepper flakes (if desired), and bring to a boil. Lower heat and simmer uncovered for 30 minutes or until chicken is tender and sauce has thickened slightly. Serve hot.

Aunt Anna's Favorite Southern-Fried Chicken

SERVES 6

2 2½- to 3-pound frying chickens, well
  washed

3 cups all-purpose flour

Salt and pepper to taste

Approximately 6 cups vegetable oil

1. Using poultry shears or a large chef's knife, cut each chicken into 12 pieces by first cutting 2 legs, 2 thighs, and 2 wings at the breast joint. Split the breasts in half and then cut each half, crosswise, into 3 small pieces. You can either use the back by cutting it into 2 pieces or freeze it to make Chicken Broth (see page 8). Rinse the chicken pieces under cold running water and pat dry.

2. Place the flour in a brown paper or plastic bag. Season with salt and pepper. Add chicken pieces, a few at a time, to the flour and shake to coat heavily. Place each well-floured piece on a wire rack to rest for at least 1 hour.

3. Heat oil in a very large, heavy skillet over medium-high heat until very hot but not smoking. Add the chicken pieces and fry, turning frequently, for about 15 minutes or until chicken is golden-brown and crispy on all sides. (Do not crowd pan; fry chicken in batches, if necessary.) About midway through the frying, season to taste with salt. Chicken is done when the point of a knife is inserted and the juices run clear.

4. As the pieces are done, remove from pan and drain on paper towels. Serve hot or at room temperature.

Chicken Scarpariello

Pollo alla Scarpariello

SERVES 6

1½ cups vegetable oil

1 pound sausage, a combination of hot and sweet, cut into bite-size pieces

2 2½-pound chickens, cut into 12 small pieces, bone in

2 large bell peppers, red, green or yellow, cored, seeded and cut, lengthwise, into ¼-inch strips

1 large yellow onion, cut, lengthwise, into ¼-inch slices

1 teaspoon minced garlic

½ cup Chicken Broth (see page 8)

½ cup dry white wine

½ cup halved Vinegared Hot Cherry Peppers (see page 9)

½ cup Vinegared Sweet Bell Peppers (see page 9)

½ cup vinegar from Vinegared Sweet Bell Peppers (see page 9)

½ teaspoon dried oregano

Salt and pepper to taste

1. Heat oil in a large, deep sauté pan over medium-high heat. Sauté sausage for about 8 minutes until lightly browned. Using a slotted spoon, remove sausage from pan and set aside to drain. Reheat oil so that it is hot but not smoking, pat chicken dry, and sauté chicken for about 15 minutes or until it is almost cooked through.

2. Stir in bell peppers, onion, and garlic and sauté for 5 minutes or until vegetables are soft and beginning to brown. Drain off all excess oil. Return sausage to pan.

3. Add wine and chicken stock to chicken, sausage, and vegetables and bring to a boil. Stir in Hot and Sweet Vinegared Peppers, vinegar, oregano, and salt and pepper. Again, bring to a boil. Lower heat and simmer slowly for about 10 minutes or until flavors have combined and sauce has reduced. Remove from heat and serve.

Note: You can, near the end of cooking, add 2 or 3 sliced boiled potatoes to this dish. Potatoes seem to have an affinity for the intense vinegar flavors, lustily absorbing the sauce.

Meats

BASICS FOR COOKING VEAL SCALLOPS

With a meat pounder or the bottom of a heavy frying pan, pound each scallop until it is thin. Right before cooking, dredge the veal in flour, shaking off excess. If you flour scallops and let them sit, the coating will be gummy and the veal will not brown properly.

If your pan is not big enough to hold all the veal without crowding, brown the veal in batches. When cooking in batches, be sure to keep the heat up to prevent the floured veal from absorbing too much oil. Brown the veal, turning once. If the oil is hot enough, this should take no more than 1 minute for floured veal, 2 minutes for battered veal.

VEAL SALTIMBOCCA

SERVES 6

12 ¹⁄₁₆-inch-thick slices prosciutto

12 veal scallops (about 1¾ pounds)

1½ cups all-purpose flour

¼ cup vegetable oil

6 tablespoons unsalted butter

1 cup Marsala wine

1 cup Chicken Broth (see page 8)

Salt and pepper to taste

1. Lay a piece of prosciutto over the top of the veal scallop. Put a piece of waxed paper over the top of each scallop and, using the side of a cleaver or the bottom of a heavy frying pan, pound the prosciutto into the veal.

2. Lightly dredge each prepared veal scallop in the flour.

3. Heat oil in a large, heavy-bottomed sauté pan over medium-high heat. Add the scallops, a few at a time, to the oil, and fry, turning once, for about 2 minutes or until veal is lightly browned. Add more oil to the pan, if necessary. Remove browned scallops to a warm serving platter.

4. When all veal has been browned, drain oil from pan.

5. Add the butter to the sauté pan and return it to medium heat. When butter has melted, stir in wine and broth, scraping up the brown bits from the bottom of the pan. Season with salt and pepper and cook for 3 minutes or until sauce has thickened slightly. Pour over the saltimbocca and serve.

VEAL MARSALA

Scaloppine al Marsala

SERVES 6

---

1 cup vegetable oil

2 cups sliced white mushrooms

Salt and pepper to taste

½ cup Chicken Broth (see page 8)

12 veal scallops (about 1¾ pounds)

1 cup all-purpose flour

3 tablespoons unsalted butter

¾ cup Marsala wine

1. Put ¼ cup oil in a medium sauté pan over medium heat. Add mushrooms, salt and pepper, and sauté for about 5 minutes or until mushrooms have exuded most of their juices and are beginning to brown. Drain off excess oil and stir in broth. Simmer for 2 to 3 minutes. Remove from heat and keep warm.

2. Heat remaining oil in a large sauté pan over medium-high heat.

3. When oil is very hot but not smoking, quickly dredge each veal scallop in flour and carefully place them into the pan. Brown each side, turning once. Using a slotted metal spatula, remove the veal to a warm platter and cover lightly. Brown remaining veal scallops.

4. When all veal has been browned, drain the oil from the pan. Return pan to medium-high heat and add butter. When butter has melted, return all scallops (with any juices) to the pan. Raise heat and pour in wine. Carefully ignite the wine and allow the flame to burn off.

5. Add the mushrooms to the veal. Season to taste with salt and pepper. Remove veal from pan and place on a warm serving plate.

6. Bring mushrooms and sauce to a boil, scraping brown bits from the bottom of the pan. Taste and adjust seasoning. Pour sauce over veal and serve.

What restaurateur wouldn't want to bottle the magic of Rao's? No other place I know of fills me with such mouthwatering anticipation upon securing a reservation, or makes me feel so fortunate upon first descending into the vestibule from the corner of 114th Street and Pleasant Avenue. And then there's Frankie. You'll never feel more at home than with this charismatic "hospitalitarian" at your tableside.

DANNY MEYER

VEAL PICCATA

Piccata di Vitello

This sauce really needs a nice tang—let your taste dictate just how much lemon juice to use.

SERVES 6

¾ cup vegetable oil

12 veal scallops (about 1¾ pounds)

1 cup all-purpose flour

3 tablespoons unsalted butter

1 cup dry white wine

½ cup Chicken Broth (see page 8)

Juice of 1 lemon

Salt and pepper to taste

1. Heat oil in a large sauté pan over medium-high heat. When oil is very hot but not smoking, quickly dredge the veal scallops in flour and carefully place them into the pan. Brown each side, turning once. As they are done, set aside on a warm platter.

2. When all scallops have been browned and removed, drain the oil from the pan. Return pan to medium-high heat and add the butter. When butter has melted, return veal (with any juices) to the pan. Raise heat and pour in wine. Bring to a boil, then add Chicken Broth and lemon juice. Stir to combine.

3. Remove veal scallops to a warm serving plate.

4. Bring sauce to a boil, scraping brown bits from the bottom of the pan. Boil for about 3 minutes or until sauce is slightly thickened. Taste and adjust seasoning with salt and pepper. Pour sauce over veal and serve.

The hardest part of moving from New York to Washington to work in the Clinton administration was leaving the wonderful food and family at Rao's. I'm delighted the president was reelected, but I still dream of the pasta with cabbage.

And whenever I'm in New York, I head straight up to 114th Street to hear Frank sing along with the jukebox, drink one of Nick's Bloody Marys, and eat some of Rao's roasted red peppers.

KATHLEEN BEGALA

VEAL FRANCESE

Vitello alla Francese

SERVES 6

---

12 veal scallops (about 1¾ pounds)

1½ cups all-purpose flour

1 recipe Seasoned Egg Batter (see page 11)

1 cup vegetable oil

1½ cups dry white wine

Juice of 1½ lemons

Salt and pepper to taste

6 tablespoons unsalted butter

1. Carefully dredge each veal scallop in flour, then in Seasoned Egg Batter. Allow excess batter to drip off. Lay coated veal scallops out on a cookie sheet, taking care not to let the edges touch.

2. Heat oil in a large sauté pan over medium-high heat. When oil is hot but not smoking, carefully place veal scallops in the pan. Brown each side, turning once.

3. Drain off all excess oil.

4. Return pan to medium-high heat and add wine, lemon juice, and salt and pepper. Bring to a boil and swirl in 2 tablespoons butter.

5. Remove scallops to a warm serving platter. Raise heat and whisk in remaining butter. When butter is well incorporated and sauce has thickened, pour sauce over veal scallops and serve.

Note: If sauce is too thick, thin with a bit of Chicken Broth (see page 8).

It was our daughter Jill's birthday and her boyfriend's initiation to the adventure of dining at Rao's. All that we had ordered for the four of us (enough to feed a table of eight) seemed to vanish quickly; and with no room left for dessert, we still caved in and ordered a wedge of ethereal cheesecake—four forks please!

Music from the jukebox spilled out over the noise and one could barely make out Pavarotti's rendition of "O Sole Mio." Suddenly the singing became louder and much clearer as we realized that a man by the name of Michael Amante from the neighboring party of eight was standing by the jukebox performing a duet with the recording. The room became silent as everyone sat mesmerized by his powerful voice. Raucous applause broke out and he was encouraged to continue and he did so a cappella, one aria after another. When the cheesecake arrived bedecked with a single candle, our daughter pleaded with her eyes not to let this gifted tenor sing "Happy Birthday," thinking it a come-down for a voice worthy of La Scala.

We will always remember the magic of this amazing happening, which could only have taken place at wonderful Rao's!

ARIE L. KOPELMAN

Of all the good folks I've sketched at table in fine eating and drinking establishments, including gambling dens, at race-tracks and golf clubhouses, etc., none, but none, nowhere, at any time gives me more satisfaction than the likeness I did of legendary owner Vincent Rao displayed next to the bar at Rao's. Vincent at the range wearing his ever-present Stetson, which served as his chef's toque, in his always welcoming open kitchen.

It is an honor having that image be the singular drawing hanging at Rao's. It is a cherished memory and I salute the picture every time upon entering the dining room.

The management's use of my art, in this complimentary way, provides a functional fulfillment of one of the nagging

Vince at Rao's '86

To Vince in Chapeau du Chef   LeRoy Neiman 86

Veal Parmigiana

Vitello alla Parmigiana

SERVES 6

1½ pounds fresh mozzarella cheese

12 veal scallops (about 1¾ pounds)

1 cup all-purpose flour

1 recipe Seasoned Egg Batter (see page 11)

2 cups Bread Crumbs (see page 11)

1 cup vegetable oil

Salt and pepper to taste

¼ cup freshly grated Pecorino Romano
   cheese

4 cups Marinara Sauce (see page 5)

1. Cut mozzarella into ¼-inch-thick slices. Set aside.

2. Carefully dredge each veal scallop in flour, then in Seasoned Egg Batter. Allow excess batter to drip off, then dredge veal in Bread Crumbs, patting the scallops to make sure that the Bread Crumbs adhere to the batter. Set aside, taking care not to let scallops overlap.

3. Preheat oven to 400° F.

4. Heat oil in a large sauté pan over medium-high heat. When oil is very hot but not smoking, carefully place veal scallops in pan. Brown each side, turning once, seasoning with salt and pepper as you turn.

5. Drain veal on paper towels. When well drained, transfer to cookie sheet(s) with sides or a large oval gratin dish.

6. Sprinkle veal with Pecorino Romano cheese. Gently overlap 3 slices of mozzarella on top of each veal scallop, lifting the cheese slightly with a fork. (This allows the cheese to puff up.) Pour Marinara Sauce into the pan so that it surrounds the veal scallops.

7. Bake for 5 minutes or until mozzarella is melted and just bubbling and beginning to brown. Spread a tablespoonful of sauce over the top and serve.

8. Put 2 veal scallops on each of 6 warm serving plates. Spoon Marinara Sauce around the veal and serve.

VEAL MILANESE

Vitello alla Milanese

SERVES 6

---

12 veal scallops (about 1¾ pounds)

1 cup all-purpose flour

1 recipe Seasoned Egg Batter (see page 11)

2 cups Bread Crumbs (see page 11)

1 cup vegetable oil

1 recipe Rao's Simple Mixed Green Salad
  (see page 35), optional

1. Carefully dredge each veal scallop in flour, then in Seasoned Egg Batter. Allow excess batter to drip off, then dredge veal in Bread Crumbs. Set coated veal scallops aside, taking care not to let the edges overlap.

2. Heat oil in a large sauté pan over medium-high heat. When oil is very hot but not smoking, carefully place veal scallops in pan. Brown each side, turning once, seasoning with salt and pepper as you turn.

3. Drain veal on paper towels. Cover lightly to keep warm.

4. Using a sharp knife, chop the salad into very fine pieces. It should be almost minced, but still crunchy.

5. Place 2 veal scallops, slightly overlapping, on each of 6 warm serving plates. Place a generous scoop of the chopped salad on each piece and serve.

Rao's is truly one of the greatest Italian restaurants. There's nothing fancy about it, just great food and great service. It must be special, because when friends of mine come into N.Y.C., most of them ask if I can get them into the restaurant. The number of tables is limited, and most of them are reserved by regular customers who come in once a week and are guaranteed their places. My good friend Charlie Cumella happens to have a table reserved for him every Wednesday. So when I'm in N.Y.C., I get to go to Rao's. Aren't I the lucky one?

VIC DAMONE

BRAISED VEAL SHANKS

Ossobuco

SERVES 6

---

7 tablespoons vegetable oil

1 large onion, finely chopped

¾ cup finely chopped carrot

¾ cup finely chopped celery

2 garlic cloves, peeled and minced

½ teaspoon freshly grated lemon zest

6 to 8 2-inch-thick slices veal shank, tied
   around the middle

2 cups all-purpose flour

1½ cups dry white wine

2½ cups Chicken Broth (see page 8)

1½ cups hand-crushed, canned, imported
   San Marzano Italian plum tomatoes

1 tablespoon minced Italian parsley

Salt and pepper to taste

1. Preheat oven to 350° F.

2. Heat 3 tablespoons oil in a large, heavy-bottomed casserole or Dutch oven over medium heat. Add the onion, carrot, and celery and sauté for about 5 minutes or until vegetables are beginning to brown. Stir in garlic and lemon zest and cook for another minute. Remove from heat.

3. Dredge the veal in the flour, shaking off any excess.

4. Heat the remaining 4 tablespoons oil in a large sauté pan. Add the veal and fry, turning once, for about 6 minutes or until meat is nicely browned. Using a slotted spoon, remove veal from pan and put on top of the vegetables in the casserole.

5. Drain oil from sauté pan and return to medium heat. Add the wine and cook, stirring frequently and scraping up the browned bits from the bottom of the pan, for about 5 minutes or until wine is slightly reduced. Pour over the veal and vegetables.

6. Add broth, tomatoes, parsley, and salt and pepper to the veal. The liquid should come up to the top of the veal. If it doesn't, add additional broth.

7. Bring casserole to a boil over medium-high heat. Remove from heat, then cover and bake in the oven, turning the veal occasionally, for about 2 hours or until the meat is almost falling off the bone and a rich, thick sauce has formed. If the sauce thickens too quickly, add water, ¼ cup at a time.

8. Remove from the oven and, using a slotted spoon, lift ossobuco from the sauce and place on a warm serving platter. Cover and keep warm.

9. Strain the sauce through a fine sieve into a saucepan. Reheat over medium heat and pour over ossobuco. Serve with rice or polenta.

BROILED VEAL CHOP

SERVES 6

6 16-ounce, 1½-inch-thick veal chops

½ cup Flavored Olive Oil (see page 10)

Salt and pepper to taste

1. Preheat broiler or grill.

2. Liberally brush each side of the chops with oil. Broil (or grill) 4 minutes on one side and then 4 minutes on the other, for rare, seasoning with salt and pepper as you turn.

3. Remove from heat and serve.

Note: You may also fry veal chops in a heavy, preferably cast-iron, skillet over very high heat for the same cooking time.

I often think of Rao's since moving from the New York area over two years ago.

I cannot think of another restaurant that my family, friends, and business associates looked forward to attending with such great anticipation.

The food and service are surpassed only by the complete dining experience you have if you are lucky enough to eat at this wonderful restaurant.

Frank, you and your family have a wonderful way of welcoming people to Rao's and maintaining that feeling throughout the dinner. It's almost like we were having dinner at your home.

On behalf of my family and all of my friends who have been lucky enough to eat at Rao's, thank you for an unbelievable dining experience.

JACK KINDREGAN

VEAL CHOP VALDOSTANO

SERVES 6

6 16-ounce, 1½-inch-thick veal chops, trimmed of all fat

18 slices prosciutto

6 tablespoons golden raisins

6 thin slices fresh mozzarella cheese

2 cups all-purpose flour

1 recipe Seasoned Egg Batter (see page 11)

1 cup vegetable oil

3 cups sliced white mushrooms

4 tablespoons unsalted butter

Approximately 3 cups Chicken Broth (see page 8)

¾ cup Marsala wine

Salt and pepper to taste

3 tablespoons chopped Italian parsley

1. Using a very sharp knife, butterfly each veal chop open horizontally to the bone, splitting the chop open like a hamburger roll. Trim all meat and fat from the handle end of the bone. Ask your butcher to chop off the top of the bone to make a neat edge. Open up the veal halves and, using the side of the cleaver or a meat pounder, pound the meat very thin.

2. Place a slice of prosciutto, then 1 tablespoon of raisins, followed by another slice of prosciutto, then a slice of mozzarella, and finally a third slice of prosciutto onto the bottom half of each chop. Pull the top half over and, using your thumb and forefinger, firmly press the top edge into the bottom. Pound the edges together.

3. Dredge the filled chops in flour, carefully shaking off any excess. Then, generously coat each side in Seasoned Egg Batter.

4. Heat oil in a large sauté pan over medium-high heat. Add the chops and fry, turning once, for about 5 minutes a side or until golden. Remove from pan and place on a warm platter.

5. Add mushrooms to the pan and sauté for about 5 minutes or until mushrooms are tender and have exuded most of their juices. Stir in butter and return chops to the pan.

6. Add broth, wine, and salt and pepper and bring to a boil. Cover and lower heat to a low simmer. Cook for about 15 minutes or until chops are very tender, adding additional broth if necessary. Remove from heat and serve, sprinkled with parsley.

BROILED STEAK

SERVES 6

6 16-ounce rib-eye steaks

½ cup Flavored Olive Oil (see page 10)

Salt and pepper to taste

1. Preheat broiler or grill.

2. Liberally brush both sides of each steak with oil.

3. Broil (or grill), for 5 minutes on each side, for rare, seasoning with salt and pepper as you turn them over.

4. At Rao's, we cut the meat from around the bone and slice the steak, on the slight diagonal, before serving. You could also serve it as is, directly from the heat.

Note: If you have a pasta first course, there is no need for starch with the steak. If not, I would suggest some Potato Croquettes (see page 150) and sautéed escarole (see page 142) as perfect accompaniments.

There is no restaurant anywhere in the world like Rao's, and dinner there every week is the greatest party in the city. It is always a Roman feast, each dish perfect, incredibly delicious, then another perfect course, and all given and received with the greatest gusto.

We have taken many people there over twenty years, from the worlds of the theater, art, and business. What we remember most is the sense of family. On entering we kiss and hug everyone: Frankie senior, Frankie junior, Nick, Anthony, everyone in the kitchen, etc., and catch up on what happened in our lives over the past week.

Then we gorge ourselves, but politely, as Frank Sinatra sings "New York, New York" and other wonderful songs.

The reaction is unanimous: "Where am I, what a fabulous evening, when can I come again, can I make a reservation for next week?" The response is always the same: "NO!"

When Stan gets up to take care of the check, our guests think it's also time for them to leave because he seems to have disappeared. They ask where he is, and invariably I have to explain that it takes as long to leave as it did to enter. Now we have to say good-bye, with hugs and kisses to everyone as before, plus anyone we may possibly have missed on the way in.

It's a great party with great hosts. Each deserves his own special thank you, which makes us doubly lucky to have our regular Tuesday night table.

CAROL AND STAN NELSON

STEAK PIZZAIOLA

Bistecca alla Pizzaiola

SERVES 6

---

1 cup vegetable oil

4 16-ounce rib-eye steaks, trimmed of all fat

3 bell peppers, cored, seeded, and cut,
   lengthwise, into ½-inch slices

2 large white onions, sliced

4 cups sliced white mushrooms

1 tablespoon minced garlic

2 cups dry white wine

4 cups hand-crushed, canned, imported San
   Marzano Italian plum tomatoes

2 pinches dried oregano

2 pinches crushed black pepper

Salt to taste

1. Heat ½ cup oil in each of 2 large sauté pans over medium-high heat. Add two steaks to each pan and fry on one side for 4 minutes or until very brown. Turn and add half of the peppers, onions, mushrooms, and garlic to each pan. Fry for an additional 4 minutes.

2. Drain off excess oil and remove steaks from the pans, leaving the vegetables. Return pans to medium-high heat.

3. Add 1 cup of wine to each pan and bring to a boil. Into each pan, stir 2 cups tomatoes, a pinch each of oregano and black pepper, and salt. Return to a boil. Lower heat and allow sauce to cook for about 5 minutes or until slightly thickened. (If sauce is too thick, thin with a bit of Chicken Broth [see page 8], using no more than ¼ cup.)

4. Return steak to sauce and allow to cook for 4 minutes. Remove from heat. Cut meat from around the bone and slice steak, on the slight diagonal, discarding the bone. Place steak on a serving platter, pour sauce over the top, and serve.

Rao's is my favorite restaurant in New York for two reasons, the first obvious, the second less so. The obvious one is the food. If I didn't know that the baked clams were made in the kitchen, I would think it possible that Frank had a special arrangement with some little-known celestial take-out operation guaranteeing instant delivery. The only problem I have with the menu is that my need to reexperience certain dishes is so urgent that I have never allowed myself to sample the full range of possibilities. Although I have been eating them for over twenty years, for example, I still can't permit a meal to pass without including pork chops with vinegar peppers.

But after the food (and this is the second reason), I go for the conversation—with Frank. Rao's has been the scene of some of the best discussions I've had in New York. For me, the evening really gets going when Frank pulls up his chair and we launch into politics, morality, movies. (In the interest of full disclosure I must point out here that Frank is unarguably the only restaurateur in the entire world who has read my book on the origins of the Boy Scout movement.) We tend to agree about a lot of things—particularly politics—but one on which we don't at all is religion. Frank is certain that there is some Supreme Being responsible for the whole business, and I am highly skeptical. He has told me that he will one day convince me. Thus far we have had only a few indecisive skirmishes, but I look forward to the dinner when he unleashes his heavy theological artillery. Suffused with the well-being provided by his clams, I'll be ready.

MICHAEL ROSENTHAL

ANNA AND FRANKIE'S MEATBALLS

Polpettini

In many southern Italian households, Sunday is meatball day. When I was a child, my father and I would steal the meatballs as fast as my mother could fry them. Yet, Mom always managed to get a plateful to the table! At Rao's, Wednesday is meatball night. When I arrive at the restaurant, the first thing I do is make off with a couple of meatballs as they are being fried in the kitchen. Guess I'm still a kid at heart!

MAKES 28

1 pound ground lean beef

½ pound ground veal

½ pound ground pork

2 large eggs

1 cup freshly grated Pecorino Romano cheese

1½ tablespoons chopped Italian parsley

½ small garlic clove, peeled and minced, optional

2 cups Bread Crumbs (see page 11)

2 cups lukewarm water

Salt and pepper to taste

1 cup fine-quality olive oil

1. Combine beef, veal, and pork in a large bowl. Add eggs, cheese, parsley, garlic, and salt and pepper to taste. Using your hands, blend ingredients together. Blend Bread Crumbs into meat mixture. Slowly add water, 1 cup at a time, until the mixture is quite moist.

2. Shape meat mixture into balls (we usually make large, 2½- to 3-inch balls).

3. Heat oil in a large sauté pan. When oil is very hot but not smoking, fry meatballs in batches. When bottom half of meatball is very brown and slightly crisp turn and cook top half. Remove from heat and drain on paper towels.

4. Lower cooked meatballs into simmering Marinara Sauce (see page 5) or Sunday Gravy (see page 65) and cook for 15 minutes. Serve over pasta or on their own.

Note: In place of Bread Crumbs, you can use stale Italian bread, white part only, that has been lightly soaked in lukewarm water.

TRIPE, ROMAN STYLE

Trippa alla Romana

SERVES 6

8 pounds fresh tripe, well cleaned

1 tablespoon salt

¾ cup olive oil

½ cup chopped prosciutto

1 cup diced onion

½ cup chopped carrot

½ cup chopped celery

1 cup dry white wine

2 cups hand-crushed, canned, imported San Marzano Italian plum tomatoes

Salt and pepper to taste

1. Put tripe in a large, heavy saucepan or Dutch oven and cover with cold water by about 3 inches. Add 1 tablespoon salt and place over high heat and bring to a boil. Lower heat and simmer for at least 1 hour or until quite tender yet almost chewy, with a firm texture. Drain and cut into ¼-inch-thick strips. Set aside.

2. Heat oil in a large saucepan over medium-high heat. Add prosciutto and sauté for 1 minute.

3. Stir in onion, carrot, and celery and sauté for 5 minutes until vegetables are soft.

4. Add wine and bring to a boil, stirring frequently. Boil for 5 minutes.

5. Stir in tomatoes and tripe. Season with salt and pepper. Bring to a boil. Lower heat and simmer for 30 minutes or until quite thick and flavors have blended. Serve with boiled, sliced potatoes.

Note: This dish only improves with time. Cook a day or two before serving and store, tightly covered and refrigerated. Reheat, adding a bit of water if sauce is too thick.

Forget the salt, don't worry about the pepper, enough with the grated cheese already. The only condiment you will ever need at Rao's is the jukebox. Certain selections on the jukebox have, over the years, become synonymous with certain selections on the menu. It's gotten so bad that I am constitutionally unable to hear these songs in any setting, anywhere in the world, without being emotionally transported to the corner of East 114th Street and Pleasant Avenue...

...Escarole and beans will forever forecast the gentle breeze of "The Summer Wind." Penne with broccoli rabe suggests the beauty of "This Bitter Earth"; for something in red, "Because of You" beckons fusilli and filetto di pomodoro. Prefer your salad before the main course? Whet your appetite with "Where or When"; brave enough to save it for after the main course, I direct you to "The Sunny Side of the Street." As you approach the main course, remember your manners. It is not polite to get up from the table until "Stardust," "I Apologize," and "I Can't Get Started With You" are completely finished, not to mention every last bite of the chicken scarpariello with hot and sweet sausages.

Finally, as you sip your espresso and pick at the cheesecake with a little fresh fruit, go with Arlene Smith and the Chantels singing "Maybe." I urge you to listen to this one most carefully of all. If you do, it might, just might, be enough to summon Aunt Anna out of the kitchen one more time to pinch you on the cheek and ask how everything was.

JONATHAN P. KAHN

What's an evening at Rao's
without music?

"My Girl"

"Up on the Roof"

"That's Amore"

"I Can't Get Started with You"

"Pretend You Don't See Her"

"Innamorata"

"In the Still of the Night"

"Rags to Riches"

"For the Longest Time"

"Just a Gigolo"

BEEF OR PORK BRACIOLA

MAKES ABOUT 10 PIECES

1 pound bottom round, cut into ¼-inch-thick slices or

1 pound lean pork, cut into ¼-inch-thick pieces

1 garlic clove, peeled and halved

1 tablespoon freshly grated Pecorino Romano cheese

1 tablespoon chopped Italian parsley

Salt and pepper to taste

1 cup fine-quality olive oil

1. Pound the meat slices thin between 2 sheets of waxed paper, using a cleaver or the bottom of a small, heavy frying pan or have your butcher pound the meat thin.

2. Rub each piece of meat with the cut side of the garlic.

3. Sprinkle each slice of meat with an equal amount of cheese and parsley. Season to taste with salt and pepper.

4. Roll the meat up, cigar-fashion, and keep firmly closed, either tied with butcher's twine or skewered with toothpicks, to keep the meat rolled while cooking.

5. Heat oil in a large sauté pan over high heat. Add the meat rolls and fry, turning frequently, for about 6 minutes or until meat is evenly browned.

6. You can now either add the Beef Braciola to Sunday Gravy (see page 65) or drain off the excess oil and add 4 cups (or enough to just cover the meat) of Marinara Sauce (see page 5). If the latter, cook for about 1 hour or until meat is very tender. Serve hot.

Broiled Pork Chops

SERVES 6

12 1½-inch-thick lean pork chops

½ cup Flavored Olive Oil (see page 10)

Salt and pepper to taste

1. Preheat broiler or grill.

2. Liberally brush both sides of each chop with oil.

3. Broil (or grill) 5 minutes on one side and 7 minutes on the other, seasoning with salt and pepper as you turn. Remove from heat and serve.

Note: You may also fry pork chops in a heavy, preferably cast-iron, skillet over very high heat for the same cooking time.

Pork Chops with Vinegared Hot and Sweet Peppers

SERVES 6

1½ cups vegetable oil

12 1½-inch-thick lean pork chops

2 garlic cloves, peeled

1 cup dry white wine

1 cup Vinegared Hot Cherry Peppers, with
   juice (see page 9)

1 cup Vinegared Sweet Bell Peppers, with
   juice (see page 9)

Salt and pepper to taste

1. Heat ¾ cup oil in each of 2 large sauté pans over high heat. When oil is very hot but not smoking, add 6 pork chops and 1 garlic clove to each pan.

2. Fry, turning once, for about 10 minutes or until chops are nicely browned, removing garlic if it gets too brown. Remove chops from pans and drain off all excess oil.

3. Cut the cherry peppers in half and remove the seeds. Measure out ⅔ cup of the vinegar juice and set aside.

4. Return pans to medium heat. Add chops, ½ cup wine, ⅓ cup vinegar juice, and ½ cup each of Vinegared Hot Cherry and Vinegared Sweet Bell Peppers to each pan. Season with salt and pepper and cook for about 15 minutes or until chops are cooked and sauce has reduced slightly. Serve.

Note: You can also add 1 boiled, sliced potato per person when you add the peppers. However, the potatoes will absorb some of the sauce so you should add ¼ cup Chicken Broth (see page 8) with the wine.

SAUSAGE WITH PEPPERS AND ONIONS

SERVES 6

½ cup fine-quality olive oil

6 sweet Italian sausages

6 hot Italian sausages

6 frying peppers, cored, seeded, and cut, lengthwise, into 1-inch strips

2 large yellow onions, peeled and cut, lengthwise, into ½-inch-thick slices

3 garlic cloves, peeled and sliced

Salt and pepper to taste

1. Heat ½ cup oil in a large sauté pan over medium-high heat. Add sausages and fry, turning frequently, for about 10 minutes or until sausages are nicely browned.

2. Stir in peppers, onions, garlic, and salt and pepper. Lower heat and fry for 5 minutes or until vegetables are just tender. Drain off any excess oil and, if desired, remove garlic. Serve.

Note: At Rao's, we always serve 1 sweet and 1 hot sausage per person. However, you can use any combination of hot and sweet sausages that you prefer. If you don't like heat, use only sweet sausages for a different but just as delicious taste. Any leftovers can be reheated and made into really great sandwiches served on crusty Italian bread.

Broiled Lamb Chops

SERVES 6

18 baby lamb rib chops, 2 inches thick, trimmed of all excess fat

½ cup Flavored Olive Oil (see page 10)

Salt and pepper to taste

1. Preheat broiler or grill.

2. Liberally brush both sides of each chop with oil.

3. Broil (or grill) 4 minutes on one side and 4 on the other, for rare, seasoning with salt and pepper as you turn. Allow 3 chops per serving.

Roast Leg of Lamb

SERVES 6

1 6-pound leg of lamb

Salt to taste

1½ tablespoons dried rosemary

1½ cups fine-quality olive oil

2 cups chopped onions

2 cups chopped carrots

2 cups chopped celery

3 tablespoons all-purpose flour

1½ cups dry white wine

2 cups Chicken Broth (see page 8)

2 cups hand-crushed, canned, imported San
Marzano Italian plum tomatoes

Pepper to taste

1. Preheat oven to 375° F.

2. Trim the lamb of all excess fat. Generously salt and season the lamb with rosemary, pushing the seasonings into all crevices. Set aside.

3. Heat oil in a large, heavy-bottomed roasting pan over medium heat. Add the lamb and roast in preheated oven for 30 minutes.

4. Stir in the onions, carrots, and celery and roast for another 20 minutes or until vegetables are beginning to brown. Remove pan from the oven and lift the lamb on to a warm plate. Lower oven temperature to 350° F.

5. Drain the vegetables through a fine sieve, allowing all excess oil to drain off. Return drained vegetables to the pan. Stir in flour and toss to combine. Stir in the wine. Add Chicken Broth and tomatoes and stir to combine.

6. Return lamb to the pan and roast for an additional 20 minutes or until a meat thermometer, inserted into a meaty part, registers 155° F for medium.

7. Remove lamb to a warm serving platter. Pour the vegetable liquid through a fine sieve into a saucepan, pushing on the vegetables to extract all the flavorful juice. Place the gravy over medium heat and bring to a boil. Taste and adjust seasoning with salt and pepper. Remove from heat.

8. Carve the lamb and serve with Roasted Potatoes (see page 151) with the gravy on the side.

SEAFOOD

Shrimp Parmigiana

SERVES 6

---

36 extra-large shrimp, peeled, deveined, and butterflied, tails removed, patted dry

1 cup all-purpose flour

1 recipe Seasoned Egg Batter (see page 11)

1½ cups Bread Crumbs (see page 11)

1 cup vegetable oil

¼ cup freshly grated Pecorino Romano cheese

36 1-ounce pieces fresh mozzarella cheese

2 cups Marinara Sauce (see page 5)

2 tablespoons chopped Italian parsley

1. Carefully dredge each shrimp in flour, then in Seasoned Egg Batter. Allow excess batter to drip off, then dredge shrimp in Bread Crumbs, ensuring that all sides are well coated.

2. Preheat broiler.

3. Heat oil in a large sauté pan over medium-high heat. When oil is very hot but not smoking, add shrimp and fry for about 4 minutes, until they are brown and crisp on all sides. (Do not crowd pan; fry shrimp in batches, if necessary.)

4. Using a slotted spoon, remove crisp shrimp to a baking sheet with sides. Sprinkle grated cheese over the shrimp and then place a piece of mozzarella on top of each shrimp. Pour Marinara Sauce around the shrimp and drizzle a bit of the sauce over the top.

5. Broil shrimp for about 4 minutes or until cheese is golden and bubbly. Serve, sprinkled with parsley.

SHRIMP SCAMPI

SERVES 6

2 pounds large shrimp, peeled, deveined, and butterflied, with tails left on, patted dry

1 cup all-purpose flour

1 cup seasoned olive oil

1½ cups dry white wine

Approximately 1 tablespoon Worcestershire sauce, or to taste

2 tablespoons minced garlic

8 tablespoons unsalted butter

Salt and pepper to taste

Juice of 1½ lemons (optional)

½ cup Chicken Broth (see page 8)

2 tablespoons chopped Italian parsley

1. Dredge shrimp in flour, coating all sides.

2. Heat oil in a large sauté pan over high heat. When oil is very hot but not smoking, add shrimp and sauté for 2 to 3 minutes or until shrimp have just begun to brown. (Do not crowd pan; sauté shrimp in batches, if necessary.) Remove shrimp from pan and drain off all excess oil.

3. Stir in wine, Worcestershire sauce, and garlic. When well combined, whisk in 4 table-spoons butter and salt and pepper and bring to a boil. Return shrimp to pan. Stir in lemon juice and broth and return to a boil.

4. Using a slotted spoon, remove shrimp from pan to a warm serving platter.

5. Rapidly boil sauce for 2 minutes, whisking in parsley and remaining butter. Pour over shrimp and serve with crusty bread to absorb the delicious sauce.

Note: At Rao's, for scampi, we serve 7 shrimp per person. Two pounds of large shrimp should yield approximately 38 to 42 shrimp.

SHRIMP FRANCESE

Gamberi alla Francese

SERVES 6

---

2 pounds large shrimp, peeled and
   deveined, butterflied, tails removed

1½ cups all-purpose flour

1 recipe Seasoned Egg Batter (see page 11)

1 cup vegetable oil

1 cup dry white wine

Juice of 1½ lemons

Salt and pepper to taste

6 tablespoons unsalted butter

3 tablespoons chopped Italian parsley

1. Carefully dredge each shrimp in flour, then dip into Seasoned Egg Batter. Allow excess batter to drip off, then dredge in flour again. Set aside, making sure shrimp do not overlap.

2. Heat oil in a large sauté pan over medium-high heat. When oil is hot but not smoking, carefully place shrimp in pan. (Do not crowd the pan; prepare shrimp in batches, if necessary.) Brown each side, turning once. If oil is hot enough, this should take no more than 1 minute.

3. Drain off all excess oil.

4. Return pan to medium-high heat and add wine, lemon juice, and salt and pepper. Bring to a boil and swirl in 2 tablespoons butter.

5. Remove shrimp to a warm serving platter. Raise heat and whisk in remaining butter. When butter is well incorporated and sauce has thickened, pour sauce over shrimp. Sprinkle with parsley and serve.

Note: If sauce is too thick, thin with a bit of Chicken Broth (see page 8).

SHRIMP OREGANATE

In this dish, you want a definite oregano flavor, but you do not want to overpower the delicate shrimp. Use a judicious hand when adding the oregano—fresh oregano works particularly well in this preparation.

SERVES 6

2 pounds large shrimp, peeled and deveined, butterflied, tails left on, patted dry

1 cup all-purpose flour

1 cup vegetable oil

2 cups dry white wine

1 cup Chicken Broth (see page 8)

Juice of 1 lemon

2 teaspoons minced garlic

2 teaspoons chopped, fresh oregano or 1 teaspoon dried oregano

Salt and pepper to taste

½ cup freshly grated Pecorino Romano cheese

Approximately 8 tablespoons unsalted butter

1 cup Bread Crumbs (see page 11)

1. Preheat oven to 400° F.

2. Dredge shrimp in flour, patting them to make sure all sides are well coated.

3. Heat oil in a large sauté pan over high heat. When oil is very hot but not smoking, add shrimp and sauté for 3 minutes or until shrimp have just begun to brown. (Do not crowd pan; prepare shrimp in batches, if necessary.) Remove shrimp from pan and drain off all excess oil.

4. Return pan to medium-high heat. Add shrimp, wine, broth, lemon juice, garlic, oregano, and salt and pepper. Bring to a boil and cook for 1 minute.

5. Using a slotted spoon, remove shrimp from pan and place on a cookie sheet with sides. Pour sauce over the top of the shrimp.

6. Sprinkle cheese over each shrimp. Place ½ teaspoon butter on each shrimp, then generously coat the tops with Bread Crumbs.

7. Bake for 3 minutes.

8. Transfer shrimp to broiler for 1 minute or until tops are brown. Serve.

Note: At Rao's, for Shrimp Oreganate, we serve 7 shrimp per person. Two pounds of large shrimp should yield approximately 38 to 42 shrimp.

Rao's has been home for many years to a family of friends who know what family is all about. Rao's, where song and laughter linger in the air, met by the aroma of a wonderful home-cooked meal. My favorite is . . . everything: the food, the people, the joint, and Frankie and his family, who keep things the way they were.

Shrimp Marinara

SERVES 6

¼ cup fine-quality olive oil

1 tablespoon minced garlic

4 cups hand-crushed, canned, imported San
   Marzano Italian plum tomatoes

Pinch dried oregano

Salt and pepper to taste

2 pounds large shrimp, peeled and
   deveined, tails removed, patted dry

1 cup all-purpose flour

½ cup vegetable oil

1 tablespoon chopped Italian parsley

1. Heat olive oil in a large sauté pan over medium heat. Add the garlic and sauté for 2 minutes, taking care not to let garlic get too brown. Stir in tomatoes, oregano, salt and pepper. Bring to a boil. Lower heat and simmer for 20 minutes or until slightly thickened.

2. Dredge shrimp in flour, patting them to make sure all sides are well coated.

3. Heat vegetable oil in a large sauté pan over medium-high heat. When oil is very hot but not smoking, add shrimp and sauté for 3 minutes or until shrimp have just begun to brown. (Do not crowd pan; prepare shrimp in batches, if necessary.) Lightly season with salt and pepper.

4. Add shrimp to sauce and cook for an additional 3 minutes. Remove from heat and serve, sprinkled with parsley.

Note: You can also serve Shrimp Marinara as a sauce for pasta.

I am single and I do not cook. So, I eat out seven nights a week. To put it simply, Rao's is my very favorite restaurant in the city. In fact, it is my favorite restaurant in the country. I love Rao's. If I could only get a reservation twice a week, I'd be there twice a week. I'll settle for once a week. O.K., Frankie, how about once a month? I guess they don't call Frankie "Frankie No" for nothing.

NEIL LEIFER

Shrimp Fra Diavolo

SERVES 6

2 pounds large shrimp, peeled and
  deveined, butterflied, tails removed,
  patted dry
1½ cups all-purpose flour
½ cup fine-quality olive oil
6 small garlic cloves, peeled
1 cup dry white wine

¼ teaspoon dried oregano
Dried red-pepper flakes to taste
Salt and pepper to taste
4 cups hand-crushed, canned, imported San
  Marzano Italian plum tomatoes
8 fresh basil leaves, torn

1. Dredge shrimp in flour, patting them to make sure that all sides are well coated.

2. Heat oil in a large sauté pan over medium-high heat. When oil is very hot but not smoking, add shrimp and sauté for 2 minutes. Stir in garlic and sauté for an additional minute or until shrimp are just beginning to brown. (Do not crowd pan; prepare shrimp in batches, if necessary.) Remove from heat and drain off all excess oil. Set shrimp aside and keep warm.

3. Return pan and garlic to medium-high heat. Stir in wine, oregano, pepper flakes, and salt and pepper. Bring to a boil and cook for 3 minutes.

4. Stir in tomatoes and cook for 15 minutes or until sauce has thickened slightly. Stir in basil and shrimp and cook for 3 minutes. If desired, remove garlic cloves. Serve.

SHELLFISH FRA DIAVOLO

SERVES 6

3 live 1½- to 2-pound lobsters

1½ cups fine-quality olive oil

12 large shrimp, peeled and deveined, butterflied, tails removed

12 littleneck, cherrystone, or manilla clams, well washed

1½ cups dry white wine

6 tablespoons cognac

1½ teaspoons minced garlic

6 cups hand-crushed, canned, imported San Marzano Italian plum tomatoes

1 cup bottled clam juice

½ teaspoon dried oregano

Pinch dried red-pepper flakes

Salt and pepper to taste

1. Immediately prior to cooking, using a very sharp, large chef's knife, kill the lobsters quickly by severing the body from the tail. Then make quick, clean cuts down the centers of the undersides, cutting the lobsters in half, lengthwise. Then, cut the body into approximately 6 pieces. Remove and crack the claws. Remove and discard the legs and antennae. Remove and set aside the tomalley (the green-colored liver).

2. Heat oil in a large, deep Dutch oven over high heat. When oil is very hot but not smoking, add the lobster. After the lobster is seared, add shrimp and clams. Sauté for about 4 minutes or until lobster is bright red, shrimp are opaque, and clams have begun to open. Remove shellfish from the pan and drain off excess oil.

3. Return pan to medium-high heat. Stir in wine, cognac, and garlic and bring to a boil. Stir in tomatoes, clam juice, oregano, pepper flakes, and reserved tomalley and again bring to a boil. Lower heat and allow to simmer for about 10 minutes or until flavors have blended and sauce has thickened slightly. Return shellfish to the pan and cook to heat through. Taste, adjust seasoning with salt and pepper, and serve.

Broiled Fillet of Sole

SERVES 6

6 large pieces fillet of sole, about 2 pounds

3 tablespoons Flavored Olive Oil (see
  page 10)

2 tablespoons all-purpose flour

¼ cup Bread Crumbs (see page 11)

2 tablespoons butter

Salt and pepper to taste

Paprika to taste

Approximately ½ cup dry white wine or
  Chicken Broth (see page 8)

¼ cup Lemon Sauce (see page 81)

1. Preheat broiler.

2. Lightly brush each fillet with oil. Lay on a baking sheet with sides that will fit easily into the broiler. Dust with flour and sprinkle Bread Crumbs over one side of each fillet and dot with butter. Season with salt, pepper, and paprika.

3. Pour wine or broth and Lemon Sauce into the baking sheet to a depth of ⅛ inch and place under the broiler. Broil, without turning, for 4 to 5 minutes or until fish easily flakes when pierced with a fork. Remove from heat and serve.

Note: Adding liquid to the pan helps the fish retain its moisture under the intense broiler heat.

When they ask me what I think about Venice and New York, I always answer that they are not towns, but sensations.

I could say the same thing about Rao's.

Rao's is not a restaurant or a bar, but a sensation. It gives me emotions.

It is the joy of being there and finding reassuring smiles, my own home food, the warm sense of affection that only people who have worked well during a lifetime at the service of other people can give. Rao's is not Italian or American, it is a place for men simple and true. Real.

GIUSEPPE CIPRIANI

FRIED FILLET OF SOLE

SERVES 6

6 large pieces fillet of sole, about 2 pounds

1 cup all-purpose flour

1 recipe Seasoned Egg Batter (see page 11)

1½ cups Bread Crumbs (see page 11)

1 cup vegetable oil

Salt and pepper to taste

2 tablespoons chopped Italian parsley

6 fresh lemon wedges

1. Carefully dredge each fillet in flour, then dip into Seasoned Egg Batter, allowing excess batter to drip off. Dredge in Bread Crumbs, patting fillets to make sure fish is well coated on both sides.

2. Heat oil in a large sauté pan over high heat. When oil is very hot but not smoking, add the fillets. Season to taste with salt and pepper. Fry, turning once, for about 5 minutes or until coating is golden and crisp and fish has cooked through. Serve, sprinkled with parsley and garnished with fresh lemon wedges.

Whenever I want a great evening—the best food in town, a completely unique ambience, and a reservation that most of my friends can only dream of getting—I call Frankie Pellegrino. So it seemed natural, when I created a fictional alter ego named Alexandra Cooper and put her in a series of murder mysteries, that her idea of a perfect place for dinner would be Rao's, too.

LINDA FAIRSTEIN

Fillet of Sole with Fennel and White Wine

SERVES 6

2 cups sliced fresh fennel bulb

1 cup all-purpose flour

6 large pieces fillet of sole, about 2 pounds

¾ cup vegetable oil

6 tablespoons unsalted butter

1 cup dry white wine

1 cup Chicken Broth (see page 8)

Juice of 1½ lemons

Salt and pepper to taste

1. Place fennel in a small pan of rapidly boiling water. Boil for about 3 minutes or until fennel is tender but still crisp. Drain and refresh under cold running water. Pat dry.

2. Lightly dredge each side of the fish in the flour, shaking off any excess.

3. Heat oil in a large sauté pan over medium-high heat. Carefully add the fillets and fry, turning once, for about 3 minutes or until fish is golden.

4. Drain all oil from the pan. Add 2 tablespoons butter. When melted, add wine, broth, and lemon juice and bring to a boil. Lower heat and add fennel and salt and pepper. Simmer for 2 minutes.

5. Using a slotted spoon, remove fish and fennel from the pan to a large, warm serving platter. Cover to keep warm.

6. Return pan to high heat and whisk in remaining butter. Boil for about 1 minute or until sauce has thickened slightly. Pour over the fish and fennel and serve.

Swordfish Livornese

SERVES 6

6 6-ounce swordfish steaks, about ¾ inch thick

1 cup all-purpose flour

½ cup vegetable oil

3 tablespoons unsalted butter

1 teaspoon minced garlic

1 cup dry white wine

½ cup pitted, halved green olives

4 teaspoons salt-packed capers, well rinsed

5 anchovy fillets packed in oil, chopped

1 cup Marinara Sauce (see page 5)

3 bay leaves

Pinch dried oregano

1. Lightly dredge each side of the fish in the flour, shaking off any excess.

2. Heat oil in a large sauté pan over medium-high heat. Carefully add the swordfish, butter, and garlic. Fry for 1 minute. Turn and fry one minute more.

3. Add the wine, olives, capers, and anchovies and stir to blend. Stir in Marinara Sauce, bay leaves, and oregano. Simmer for 3 minutes or until flavors have blended. Remove bay leaves and serve.

Note: Because of the saltiness of the anchovies and capers, this sauce generally does not require additional seasoning.

Uncle Vincent's Christmas Eve Baccalà

8 to 10 all-purpose potatoes, peeled and quartered

1 cup fine-quality olive oil

1 bunch celery, trimmed, well-washed, and cut into 3-inch-long pieces

1 large onion, chopped

2 cups Gaeta olives

4 28-ounce cans hand-crushed, San Marzano imported Italian plum tomatoes, with juice

12 cups Chicken Broth (see page 8)

4 pounds dried salt cod, cut into 3-inch pieces, soaked (see page 39)

Salt to taste

1. Place potatoes in cold water to cover over high heat. Bring to a boil and cook for about 15 minutes or until potatoes are almost cooked through. Drain.

2. Heat oil in a large, heavy-bottomed casserole over medium heat. Add the celery and sauté for about 5 minutes, then add onion and sauté until vegetables begin to get soft. Add the olives and sauté for an additional minute. Stir in the tomatoes and their juice. Bring to a boil. Lower heat and simmer for 10 minutes.

3. Stir in broth and return to simmer.

4. Stir in the potatoes and the soaked baccalà and simmer for about 10 minutes or until the potatoes are cooked and the baccalà flakes when poked with a fork.

5. Taste and, if necessary, add salt. Serve hot.

Note: Often, salt cod dishes will require no additional salt. Therefore, always taste before adding any seasoning.

Vegetables

Rao's Four Basic Vegetables

The preparation of Rao's four standard vegetables is a specialty of Annie Sausto's. She seems to be able to bring the deepest flavor from these menu basics.

Each of the following portions will be enough for 6 people, sautéed, or sufficient to add to pasta or sauces as required in any recipe in this book.

BROCCOLI RABE

Broccoli di Rape

2 large bunches broccoli rabe

1. Remove any tough outer or damaged leaves. Cut off the stems and tear the leaves into large pieces (about 3 to 4 inches). Wash in a sink filled with cold water. Shake off excess water.

2. Place broccoli rabe in a deep saucepan with cold water to cover by about 2 inches. Bring just to a simmer over high heat. As soon as bubbles appear at the sides of the pan, remove it from the heat.

3. Drain cooking water. (Reserve it if you are going to combine the broccoli rabe with pasta or are going to prepare a Rao's recipe requiring broccoli rabe water.)

4. Immediately place broccoli rabe in cold water to cover to stop the cooking process. When broccoli rabe is cool, drain well in a colander and pat dry.

5. Cover with a damp cloth and refrigerate until ready to sauté or add to pasta or sauces.

Need I say we will miss you? But I suspect that is an integral part of our existence: In America we missed our Russian friends, in Russia we'll miss our American friends, and in both countries we miss our French friends. But having fully experienced the pain and frustration of not being free to travel, we rejoice in the knowledge that we can pick up and go whenever we wish—and host you, should you desire to visit us in Moscow.

VLADIMIR AND KATHERINE POZNER

SAVOY CABBAGE

1 large Savoy cabbage

1. Cut cabbage, lengthwise, into 6 pieces. Wash well in a sink filled with cold water. Shake dry.

2. Put cabbage in a large saucepan with cold water to cover by 2 inches and bring to a boil over high heat. Lower heat and simmer for 5 minutes.

3. Drain in a colander and run under cold water to stop the cooking process. Allow to drain well and pat dry.

4. Cover with a damp cloth and refrigerate until ready to sauté or add to pasta or sauces.

ESCAROLE

Scarola

2 large bunches escarole

1. Remove any tough outer or damaged leaves from the escarole. Cut off the tough root end and tear leaves into large pieces. Wash well in a sink filled with cold water. Shake off excess water.

2. In a deep saucepan with cold water to cover by about 2 inches, boil escarole for 5 minutes over high heat.

3. Remove from heat and drain in a colander. Immediately place escarole in cold water to cover to stop the cooking process. When escarole is cool, drain well in a colander and pat dry.

4. Cover and refrigerate until ready to sauté or add to pasta.

BROCCOLI

1 large head broccoli, approximately 2 pounds

1. Trim the broccoli. Cut off florets into approximately 1-inch pieces. Wash well.

2. In a large saucepan, with cold water to cover by about 2 inches, boil broccoli over high heat for about 4 minutes or until water turns green and broccoli is crisp-tender.

3. Drain into a colander and immediately rinse under cold running water.

4. When broccoli is cold, pat dry.

5. Cover with a damp cloth and refrigerate until ready to sauté or add to pasta.

Like being home—without the angst.

BILLY SQUIER

Garlic-and-Oil-Sautéed Vegetables

SERVES 6

½ cup Flavored Olive Oil (see page 10)

4 garlic cloves, peeled and minced

1 recipe broccoli rabe (see page 138), or
Savoy cabbage (see page 140), or escarole
(see page 140), or broccoli (see page 141)

Salt and pepper to taste

1. Heat oil in a large, heavy sauté pan over medium heat. Add garlic.

2. Stir in the vegetable and sauté for 3 minutes or until hot. Season with salt and pepper and serve.

Note: Take care not to brown the garlic or vegetables will taste bitter.

Peas and Prosciutto

SERVES 6

¼ cup Flavored Olive Oil (see page 10)

½ cup finely chopped onion

½ cup diced prosciutto

2 15-ounce cans green peas, drained, or
2 cups fresh peas, cooked

1 cup Chicken Broth (see page 8)

Salt and pepper to taste

1. Heat oil in a large sauté pan over medium heat.

2. Add onion and sauté for 3 minutes or until translucent. Stir in the prosciutto and sauté for an additional 3 minutes.

3. Add the peas, broth, and salt and pepper. Cook for about 3 minutes or until hot.

4. Drain off all liquid and serve.

SAUTÉED MUSHROOMS

SERVES 6

½ cup fine-quality olive oil

2 garlic cloves, peeled

1½ pounds fresh white mushrooms (or a mixture of white and wild mushrooms), sliced

¼ cup dry white wine

Salt and pepper to taste

2 tablespoons chopped Italian parsley

1. Heat oil in a large sauté pan over medium heat. Add garlic and sauté for 3 minutes or until golden. Remove and discard garlic.

2. Add mushrooms and sauté for about 5 minutes or until tender but still firm. Add the wine and salt and pepper. Bring to a boil and cook for 1 minute.

3. Remove from heat and stir in parsley. Serve hot or at room temperature.

Note: If you can find very small mushrooms, leave them whole.

FRANKIE'S ARTICHOKES

SERVES 6

6 large artichokes

Juice of 1 lemon

1 lemon, halved

1½ cups Bread Crumbs (see page 11)

½ cup freshly grated Pecorino Romano
   cheese

1 tablespoon chopped Italian parsley

Salt and pepper to taste

1 cup fine-quality olive oil

1 clove crushed garlic

1. Submerge the artichokes in cold water and agitate the water with your hands so that the artichokes are cleansed of all debris.

2. Squeeze the juice of one lemon into a bowl of cold water. Set aside.

3. One at a time, tear off and discard the tough outer leaves of each artichoke by pulling down and away from the center until they snap off. While you work with each artichoke, constantly rub it with a cut lemon half to keep it from darkening. Using a paring knife, neatly cut off the stalk and trim the area where you have removed the leaves. Using a sharp knife, cut off about one quarter of the top of each artichoke. Using kitchen shears, cut off the tips of all the remaining leaves to make an even shape. Turn the trimmed artichoke upside down and push and roll it to cause the entire flower to open up. As each artichoke is finished, put it in the lemon water.

4. Combine Bread Crumbs, cheese, parsley, garlic, and salt and pepper. Set aside.

5. Place two clean kitchen towels on a flat surface. Remove artichokes from the lemon water and turn upside down on the towels to drain.

6. When artichokes are well drained, pat dry. Place an equal portion of the Bread Crumb mixture into the center and between every leaf of each artichoke, or loosely sprinkle Bread Crumb mixture into and on top of artichokes.

7. Put 1 inch of water, 1 tablespoon salt, and ½ cup oil in a heavy-bottomed casserole large enough to hold the artichokes in a single layer. Add the artichokes, stem side down. Drizzle with remaining oil. Cover and bring to a simmer over high heat. Lower heat and allow arti-

chokes to steam for about 45 minutes or until artichoke bottoms are tender when pierced with the tip of a sharp knife. If water evaporates to less than ½ inch before artichokes are cooked, add additional water (and oil, if desired).

8. Using tongs, carefully remove artichokes from water, reserving pan juices. Pour pan juices into six individual soup bowls and place artichokes in the center. Serve hot.

What is Rao's?

A kaleidoscope of delicious moments that fall into an ever-changing collage of memories:

> *of mahogany booths*
>
> *of a pressed-tin ceiling*
>
> *of year-round Christmas lights*
>
> *of Nicky behind his bar*
>
> *of Franky Nazzo and Johnny Roast Beef*
>
> *of locals and celebrities*
>
> *of walls of photos and Angelo's diploma*
>
> *of a sentiment-stuffed jukebox with endless Sinatra*
>
> *of a fish tank with a solitary deep-sea diver, but no fish*
>
> *of pounds of De Cecco pasta on a shelf in the kitchen*
>
> *of Anna and Vincent before a large Garland stove, she wearing a white silk blouse, he with a leather ten-gallon hat*
>
> *of Frankie singing side-by-side with the Ink Spots in a mellow mood at the end of an evening*
>
> *of roasted peppers, seafood salad, broccoli rabe, and penne*
>
> *of scarpariello and lemon chicken and ecstasy, and dreams and memory.*

JUDY ROSENTHAL

Asparagus with Parmigiano-Reggiano Cheese

2 pounds fresh asparagus

Salt to taste

6 tablespoons unsalted butter, melted

1 cup freshly grated Parmigiano-Reggiano cheese

1. Preheat oven to 400° F.

2. Trim the tough ends from the asparagus. Peel off the tough skin from around the bottom of the stalks. Lay the cleaned asparagus flat in a pan. Add cold water to cover by 1 inch and salt. Bring to a boil over medium-high heat. Cover. Lower heat and simmer for 4 minutes or until asparagus is just tender but still firm. Drain well and pat dry.

3. Arrange asparagus, tips in the same direction, into 6 servings on a baking sheet with sides. Drizzle butter over each bundle and generously sprinkle cheese over all.

4. Bake in preheated oven for 5 minutes or until cheese has melted. Carefully lift each bundle from the pan using a large spatula and serve.

Note: For a very luxurious dish, stack the asparagus bundles in layers, placing a generous portion of grated cheese between each layer.

Sometimes a restaurant can become a "second home." Actually, our second home is in New York, and whenever we're there, we can't wait to go to Rao's. Frankie and his crew not only make us feel at home, but serve absolutely great food. A visit to Rao's is truly a memorable event.

DICK CLARK

POTATO CROQUETTES

MAKES 12

3 tablespoons plus 4 cups vegetable oil

½ cup finely chopped onion

½ cup finely chopped prosciutto

1 pound all-purpose potatoes, cooked and mashed

3 large egg yolks

½ pound fresh mozzarella cheese, finely chopped

¼ pound freshly grated Pecorino Romano cheese

1 tablespoon finely minced Italian parsley

Salt and pepper to taste

2 cups Bread Crumbs (see page 11)

1½ cups all-purpose flour

3 whole eggs

1. Heat 3 tablespoons oil in a medium sauté pan over medium-high heat. Stir in the onion and prosciutto and sauté for 5 minutes. Remove from heat.

2. Place potatoes in a large mixing bowl. Add onions and prosciutto and, using a wooden spoon, beat together.

3. Beat in egg yolks, cheeses, and parsley. Taste and adjust seasoning with salt and pepper.

4. Using your hands, shape potato mixture into 12 logs of equal size. Set aside.

5. Place Bread Crumbs in a wide, shallow bowl and season with salt and pepper.

6. Place flour in a wide, shallow bowl.

7. Place eggs in another wide, shallow bowl and whisk with a fork until well blended.

8. Carefully dredge each potato log in the flour. Dip into the eggs and then dredge in seasoned Bread Crumbs, taking care that logs are well coated. Place on a cookie sheet and set aside.

9. Heat remaining oil in a deep-fat fryer to 365° F. Carefully lower logs into the oil, a few at a time, and fry for about 2 minutes or until golden. Drain on paper towels and serve.

Note: Potato Croquettes may be prepared early in the day and stored, covered and refrigerated. Fry just before serving.

ROASTED POTATOES

At Rao's, we serve these crisp, rosemary-flavored potatoes with steaks and chops. At home, they would be terrific served with roasts as well.

SERVES 6

2 pounds all-purpose potatoes

Salt to taste

⅓ cup Flavored Olive Oil (see page 10)

1 teaspoon dried rosemary

Pepper to taste

1. Preheat oven to 375° F.

2. Peel potatoes and cut them in half.

3. Place potatoes in a large saucepan with cold water to cover by about 2 inches. Add salt. Bring to a boil over high heat. Lower heat and simmer for 5 minutes or until just beginning to cook. Remove from heat and drain well. Pat dry.

4. Place potatoes in a baking dish and drizzle with oil. Add rosemary and salt and pepper to taste. Toss to coat well. Roast in preheated oven for 25 minutes or until outside is crisp and golden-brown. Serve hot.

Sweets

Fresh Fruit

In Italy, sweets are associated with celebrations, festivals, or saint's days, and are eaten only on special occasions. Fresh fruit is the dessert of choice. At Rao's, we continue this tradition with our most popular dessert being, quite simply, a plate of fresh fruit. Winter or summer, we always have a variety of ripe, seasonal fruits on hand. Large fruit, such as melons or pineapple, is usually quartered or sliced. Smaller fruits are most often served whole. If you choose to cut the fruit before serving, it is important that it be carefully trimmed and beautifully arranged on the plate. No matter how you present it, the fruit should be perfectly ripe and sweet.

CHEESECAKE

MAKES 1 CAKE

¼ cup Bread Crumbs (see page 11)

1 pound ricotta cheese

1 pound cream cheese

6 large eggs

1¼ cups sugar

2 teaspoons pure vanilla extract

1 teaspoon freshly grated lemon zest

2 cups sour cream

1. Preheat oven to 350° F.

2. Lightly butter a 9-inch springform pan and coat it with Bread Crumbs, shaking out any excess.

3. Press the ricotta through a fine sieve and combine it with the cream cheese in the large bowl of an electric mixer. Beat, on medium speed, for 5 minutes or until very smooth. Add eggs, one at a time, and beat until well incorporated. Add 1 cup sugar, 1½ teaspoons vanilla, and lemon zest, and beat for 3 minutes or until very light and smooth.

4. Pour into prepared pan. Bake in preheated oven for 1 hour or until cake is set in the center. If edges begin to brown, lower heat to 300° F and add about 15 additional minutes of baking time. Remove from oven but leave heat on.

5. Beat together sour cream, remaining sugar, and vanilla. When well blended, generously coat top of cake. Return to oven and bake for 10 minutes.

6. Remove from oven and cool on wire rack.

7. When cool, remove from springform pan to a chilled serving plate. Refrigerate until ready to serve.

From Joey and Vince, to Annie and Frankie "No" . . . A hundred years of great dining moments! From memories of my first date in the rear booth, to my mom singing doo-wop . . . Rao's has always maintained that wonderful blend of excellent food and enjoyment in an atmosphere filled with its own special history. From the neighborhood pals, to the cops I worked with, to the many people in the entertainment world who have been my guests at Rao's—two things I always hear: the first is, "It's one of the best nights I've ever had!" and the second is, "What the hell are all those Christmas lights still doing up all over the place?"

SONNY GROSSO

My earliest recollections of Rao's are that it was a very special place. When I was a child, it was a great treat for my dad to take me down the "hole," as it was affectionately called, and let me sit at the bar for a Coke. This usually occurred during the feast and added to the fun and excitement. There were lots of adults around having fun and always a dog or two. To me Rao's always seemed like an ongoing party. It was part of my childhood, much like a wonderful neighbor welcoming you in. Today I take my children to Rao's and I watch them experience that same sense of excitement, and I am so happy to be able to share with them a piece of my childhood.

SUSAN RIENZI PAOLERCIO

TIRAMISU

MAKES 1 CAKE

6 large eggs

1 cup granulated sugar

½ cup Kahlúa, brandy, or other liqueur

4½ cups mascarpone cheese

1 cup tiny chocolate bits and/or ½ cup diced,
   glazed orange peel

3 cups boiling water

3 tablespoons light brown sugar

3 tablespoons instant espresso powder

1 tablespoon fine-quality cocoa powder

2 7-ounce packages Champagne biscuits
   (see Note)

½ cup grated bittersweet chocolate

1. Whisk eggs and sugar together in a heat-proof bowl over a pan of simmering water, but do not allow it to touch the water. Using a handheld electric mixer, beat for approximately 7 minutes or until mixture has tripled in volume and a candy thermometer inserted into it reads 160° F. Remove bowl from pan.

2. Beating constantly, add liqueur 1 tablespoon at a time. Continue beating for about 5 minutes or until mixture is cool.

3. When cool, beat in mascarpone until well blended. If using, stir in chocolate bits and/or fruit. Cover and refrigerate for 1 hour or until well chilled.

4. Combine water, brown sugar, espresso powder, and cocoa in a medium bowl. Stir until espresso powder and cocoa dissolve.

5. One at a time, completely dip biscuits into the espresso mixture, then put them in the bottom of a 13 × 9 × 2-inch glass baking dish to completely cover the bottom. If necessary, cut biscuits to fit.

6. Evenly spread one third of the mascarpone mixture over the biscuits. Continue dipping and layering, making 2 additional layers of biscuit and mascarpone, ending with a cheese layer.

7. Tightly cover with plastic wrap and refrigerate for at least 8 hours.

8. When ready to serve, sprinkle grated chocolate over the top. Cut into squares and serve cold.

Note: Champagne biscuits are 4-inch-long cookies similar to lady fingers that are available at Italian markets, specialty food stores, and some supermarkets. If you can't find them, you can substitute traditional lady fingers.

CANNOLI

MAKES ABOUT 16

1 cup all-purpose flour

4 tablespoons sugar

¼ teaspoon salt

1 tablespoon unsalted butter, softened

¼ cup dry white wine

Approximately 4 cups vegetable oil

2 cups ricotta cheese

1 cup heavy cream, whipped

1½ teaspoons pure vanilla extract

2 tablespoons finely minced candied fruit

½ cup tiny semisweet chocolate bits

1. Combine flour, 1 tablespoon sugar, and salt in a mound on a clean, flat surface. Make a well in the center and cut small pieces of the butter into it. Pour the wine into the well and, using a fork, pull the flour into the wine, stirring until most of the flour is incorporated. Using your hands, knead until smooth, picking up any remaining flour as you knead.

2. On a clean, lightly floured surface, roll out the dough to about ¹⁄₁₆ inch thick. Cut dough into 3½-inch squares.

3. Lay cannoli forms diagonally across the center of each square. If you don't have cannoli forms, use any heat-proof cylinder that is at least 1 inch in diameter. Wrap pastry up and around the form with the corners overlapping in the center. Firmly press corners together. If pastry does not stick, moisten corners with a tiny amount of water and press to hold.

4. Heat oil to 375° F on a candy thermometer in a large, deep sauté pan over high heat.

5. Add the cannoli, no more than 3 at a time, as pastry swells quickly, and fry, carefully turning, for about 2 minutes or until pastry is crisp, golden, and slightly blistered.

6. Carefully remove forms from oil and gently push pastry off forms and onto paper towels to drain. Take great care as both forms and pastry are very hot. Continue frying until all the pastry is cooked.

7. When well drained, remove to wire racks to cool.

8. In a mixing bowl, beat ricotta until light. Fold in remaining sugar, whipped cream, vanilla, and candied fruit until well blended.

9. Using a narrow spatula or bread knife, fill cannoli shells, one end at a time, making sure that the center is filled. Smooth off the ends and dip each end into chocolate bits. Serve immediately.

Note: Cannoli shells can be fried and filling made early in the day, but they must be filled just before serving or the shells will get soggy.

If you don't have the time to make them, prepared cannoli shells are available in Italian markets, specialty food stores, and some supermarkets.

ALMOND BISCOTTI

MAKES ABOUT 3 DOZEN

2½ cups sifted all-purpose flour

1 tablespoon baking powder

½ teaspoon salt

¼ teaspoon ground mace

4 tablespoons unsalted butter, at room
  temperature

¾ cup sugar

½ teaspoon freshly grated lemon zest

1 teaspoon pure vanilla extract

½ teaspoon almond extract

2 large eggs

1 cup coarsely chopped, toasted blanched
  almonds

1. Preheat oven to 375° F.

2. Cover a large cookie sheet with parchment paper or aluminum foil. Set aside.

3. In a medium bowl, sift together flour, baking powder, salt, and mace. Set aside.

4. Using an electric mixer, beat butter until light and creamy. Add sugar and continue beating until light and fluffy. Beat in lemon zest, vanilla, and almond extract. Add eggs, one at a time, beating to incorporate.

5. Stir in flour mixture and almonds until well blended. If necessary, knead by hand to make a smooth dough.

6. Divide dough in half and mold each half into a strip about 12 inches long and 2½ inches wide. Place the strips, 4 inches apart, on the prepared cookie sheet.

7. Bake in preheated oven for 18 minutes or until pale gold but not brown. Remove from oven and let cool on wire racks.

8. Lower oven temperature to 300° F.

9. Place cooled strips on a flat cutting surface and, using a serrated knife, cut crosswise into ½-inch-wide slices. Place slices on cookie sheet.

10. Return cookies to oven and bake for 10 minutes. Turn and continue to bake for an additional 10 minutes. Turn off oven and open door. Allow biscotti to cool in the oven with the door open.

11. Store, tightly covered, for up to 3 weeks.

Amaretti

MAKES ABOUT 5 DOZEN COOKIES

8 ounces almond paste

1 cup granulated sugar

2 teaspoons almond extract

4 large egg whites

Pinch salt

¼ cup confectioners' sugar

1. Preheat oven to 300° F.

2. Using an electric mixer, beat together the almond paste, sugar, and extract. Add 1 egg white and continue beating until smooth.

3. In a separate bowl, beat remaining egg whites until foamy. Add salt and continue beating until stiff but not dry.

4. Fold the beaten egg whites into the almond paste mixture and then beat for about 3 minutes or until very light.

5. Lightly butter and flour 3 cookie sheets. Drop the batter by the half teaspoonful on to the prepared cookie sheets, leaving about 1½ inches between cookies.

6. When all cookies are made, place confectioners' sugar into a fine sieve and gently shake it over the cookies so each cookie is lightly covered. Let rest for 1½ hours.

7. Bake cookies in the preheated oven for 20 minutes or until golden-brown. Remove from oven and allow to cool on the cookie sheets.

8. Store, tightly covered, in separated layers, for up to 2 weeks.

Rao's, quite simply, serves the best Italian food, in the most fun atmosphere, on the planet. Bar none.

ROB REINER

I had just published the paperback edition of Umberto Eco's The Name of the Rose *and Umberto was in town to promote it, so I decided to take him and a few other friends up to Rao's, always our special place. Of course, we had three generous courses and then dessert and coffee with "holy water" liberally added by the great Nick the Vest. To start off we had had a couple of drinks to get us ready for the meal. Obviously, a few bottles of white and red were needed to lubricate the proceedings. Frankie, always the generous host, insisted that we cap off the evening with some grappa on him. Well, we all wound up dancing to the great Rao's jukebox and, not for the first time, closed the place. As we were leaving Umberto turned and said to me, "Howard, that was the best evening in a restaurant I've ever had, but I think I forgot something." "What did you forget, Umberto?" I asked him. "The title of my book! I'm thinking now it might be* The Name of the Fish Salad *or maybe even* The Name of the Grappa. *Well, whatever it is, that was some dinner!"*

HOWARD KAMINSKY

Rao's! The toast of the town where cognoscenti, world tourists, and friends scramble for impossible reservations. The home cooking, which for some was an epicurean discovery, coupled with the restaurant's fascinating history, makes Rao's a must for diners everywhere.

MARIO BIAGGI

ACKNOWLEDGMENTS

Let me first acknowledge David Vigliano and Ed Breslin, two extraordinary literary agents who came to me one evening at the restaurant in the summer of 1996 with a proposal to do a Rao's cookbook. At first I was reluctant; I wasn't sure if I could really do the project justice, or if I was willing to commit myself to such a formidable task, or if I wanted the kind of pressure and publicity associated with the publishing of a book. But I knew in my heart that Rao's deserved a book. Any restaurant that could last one hundred years in the same location, with the same family, deserved some kind of testament to its existence, simply for the sake of posterity. More important, I wanted to pay tribute to Vincent and Anna Pellegrino Rao for what they had accomplished. Vincent loved his restaurant and his neighborhood. Aunt Anna devoted her life to Vincent and spent the last twenty years of her life making the Rao's kitchen famous. It is because of them that Rao's exists today. It is because of them that anyone would even want a Rao's cookbook. Hence, all of my trepidation aside, we have a cookbook.

I would like to thank Jason Epstein of Random House for giving the project a green light. (Little did I know that Jason is a gourmet chef and just wanted the recipes for himself.) Thank you, Jason.

I'd also like to thank Joy de Menil, Kathy Rosenbloom, and Benjamin Dreyer of Random House for their keen interest and valuable suggestions as the project went along.

I'd like to thank Judith Choate and her husband for putting together the first draft of the recipes. They spent long hours in our kitchen, working diligently with our entire staff to get this project under way.

I'd like to say something about my "aunt" Annie Sausto, a lifelong friend to Vincent and Anna Rao and to me. She is our next-door neighbor and has been working in Rao's for more than twenty years. She is eighty years old now and opens the restaurant every morning. She calls the purveyors and orders what we need for the day. She washes the vegetables, she cleans the fish, she roasts the peppers, she starts the sauce. She is the mother hen and keeps everyone in line. I do not know what I would do without her.

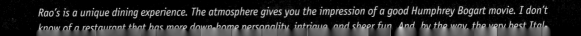

Rao's is a unique dining experience. The atmosphere gives you the impression of a good Humphrey Bogart movie. I don't know of a restaurant that has more down-home personality, intrigue, and sheer fun. And, by the way, the very best Ital-

Besides including recipes, we wanted the book to talk about history and family, which is the real fabric of which Rao's is woven—it is what gives Rao's its depth and texture and reason for being. Enter Nicholas Pileggi, a friend, a customer, a gentleman, and a masterful writer. Soon after I was approached to do this book, I called Nick and asked if he would write the text for this book. He immediately said yes. I was thrilled, and so was Random House. Thank you, Nick, for your talent, your friendship, and your contribution to this book.

You might think by now I had all the help I needed, but lo and behold, who comes in and writes another ten pages of humorous and joyful text but another good friend and customer, the sportswriter Dick Schaap. Dick and his wife, Trish, have been customers for years, and I can't tell you how happy I am that Dick is a part of this book.

I'd like to pay special thanks to my cousin Susan. A native of East Harlem and a champion of Italian culture, Susan researched much of the historical data for the text, and she is generally responsible for keeping my business life in order.

How much is a picture worth? In this book, the photography is priceless. The photos of the restaurant and of the food were taken by a young genius by the name of Stephen Hellerstein. Along with the direction and ideas of Sebastian Nick LaMicela and Frank Pellegrino, Jr., Hellerstein's photographs capture explicitly the history, the warmth, the story, the flavor, and the people that are Rao's. I must also thank Mr. LaMicela for getting the world-famous photographer Hiro to take the picture of me that is included in this book. Thank you, Hiro, for the honor.

Ten months into the project, when we weren't anywhere near done, I started to feel that we would never get it all together and that Random House would lose interest. Random House must have felt the same way, because they decided to send an editor by the name of Susan DiSesa to get this book finished. Susan was exactly the angel we needed. She pulled the book together, assembling all its parts. She worked with me in reediting and fine-tuning all the recipes and all the text. For the first time since starting the project, I finally felt we were not only going to get it done, but it was going to be exactly the book I envisioned: something unique and special. Susan, I could not have finished this book without you.

I would like to thank Georgiana Goodwin, book designer extraordinaire. Georgiana is a sincere and dedicated professional who worked under great pressure to design this book in a way that would make everyone happy. I thank you, Georgiana, for your patience, your professionalism, and your artistry.

Ron Straci is a member of the Rao family. He is Vincent Rao's nephew and my partner at Rao's. Ron's contribution of family photos and eloquent remembrances is invaluable not only for their charm but for the authenticity they give this work. Amid all the chaos, Ron is always there to support me with perspective and sage advice. Thank you, Ron.

I'd like to pay tribute to the staff at Rao's. A restaurant is only as good as the people who work there. I love my staff. What's more important, my *customers* love my staff. There are no pretensions. What you see is what you get. Nicky "the Vest" Zaloumis has been with us forever. He is the best mixologist in New York. Anthony "Yin Yang" Silvers is a real character—ponytail and all—but my customers adore him. I'd also like to thank Little Tommy, a fine young man with a great sense of humor; everyone in the kitchen: Eddie, Dominick, Lydia, and Dino; and a special thanks to my head chef, Mario Curko, who worked with me and the food editors in putting all the recipes together. Thanks, gang.

A special tribute and thank you to my son, Frank junior. Frank started working at Rao's fourteen years ago, when he was fourteen years old, as a busboy. He now manages the restaurant. We have all had the pleasure of watching him grow into a talented young man with an advertising agency of his own. He continues to work with me at the restaurant simply because he knows I need his help. How lucky can a father get? Thank you, son.

To all of our loyal customers at Rao's: I wouldn't trade you for the clientele of any other restaurant anywhere in the world. Your loyalty, your love, and your respect I have seen nowhere else in my life. You have educated me, you have supported me, you have respected me. Except for my wife and my two children, you have given me my greatest sense of accomplishment. More than anything, *you* are what has made Rao's legendary. Thank you.

One last tribute: to my wife, Josephine, and my daughter, Angela. You truly are the wind beneath my wings.

Thank you, everyone.
Frankie

BIG T • BEGALA • MRS. HANRAHAN • JOHNNY CIGARS • JOHNNY ROASTBEEF • ANGELO URGITANO • DR. KOSOVSKY • MARIETTA • BON-JOVI • DEBBIE BANNER • STEVE WITKOFF • CAROL NELSON • CHARLIE KOPPLEMAN • BILLY CRYSTAL • JUSTIN FELDMAN • EMILY COHEN • DOMINICK RAVIOLI • KATE COTE • DANNY HIRSCH • ACE GREENBERG • PHIL GREENWALD • ED SUMMERFELD • TONY ABBOTT • JACK COWLON • JACK KINDREGAN • ALBA BRIGNOLI • ANTHONY QUINN • FRANKIE NOSE • PETEY NECK • RON ROSA • ANTHONY CANTARELLA • ROB REINER • LOU LINDER • STAN NELSON • ROBERT SUMMER • LINDA FAIRSTEIN • ARIE KOPELMAN • DICK GRASSO • EDWIN TORRES • DAN COHEN • PETER ARDITO • SUSAN GELMAN • PETER BROCK • BOB CORMAN • BILL ROLLNICK • NANCY ELLISON • DAVID PECKER • BRUNO KIRBY • SUSAN KASEN • JERRY FERRARI • JOHNNY BLUE • LITTLE JERRY • TOMMY T. • RED JUKE BOX • PINTO • ARTIE DeMICHAEL • CINDY CRAWFORD • BRENDA VACCARO • SONNY GROSSO • JONATHAN KAHN • MIKE MANZA • JOHN DeGREGORIO • RON PERELMAN • ARCHIE SINUK • LOUIS PACELLA • FRAN DRESCHER • FATHER PETE • ANDRE AGASSI • RUSTY STAUB • LARRY PERSE • DENNIS STEIN • CARMINE DELLACAVA • JIMMY LeCERRA • SENATOR D'AMATO • BROOKE SHIELDS • LINDA BEAUCHAMP • JOEY HUNTER • LARRY SCHWARTZ • KRISTEN JENSON • JACK SCALIA • KIM HUNTER • AL PACINO • REGIS PHILBIN • LEN CARIOU • DONNA KARAN • KAL RUTENSTEIN • SENATOR DODD • MARY HIGGINS CLARK • JIMMY CIGARS • JOHN KENNEDY, JR. • PETER KRIENDLER • BILLY VERA • CIRO DENETTIS • WENDY • BOTH ROBBINS • LORI • ARLENE • DEVI • CATHERINE • SONNY AQUINO • ANTHONY 114 • EDDIE GERMANO • JUDY ROSENTHAL • DR. CIAFA • DR. SIEGEL • JOE BANNER • DR. BERGER • JIM BOZART • DAVID • MICHAEL ROSENTHAL • FATHER VINCI • FATHER RORANO • JOHN COLTON • NOHA HASSAN • TODD GARRETT • PHIL SIMMS • PHIL McCONKEY • THE MORMONDOS • SALLY MILANO • DR. FRIED • UNCLE JOHN • CARMINE LATERRA • JOHN POGGI • JODY KAHN • ROBERT DeNIRO • MARTIN SCORSESE • THE JET • LOUIS CARCATERRA • HENRY MARKS • STEVE SIEGEL • MARK COHEN • NEIL SROKA • BROTHER DAVID • FORTGANG • LANZARRO • CHARLIE CUMELLA • GUCCIONE • TAGLIATELLA • DR. CASAS • HOLDSTEIN • GENE ORZA • STAN MARX • ED McCABE • SUSAN MAGRINO • MITTMAN • BILLY SQUIER • KAPNICK • RIBELLINO • FELDMAN • WACHMAN • PARDEE • FIANO • BRENT • MADONNA • MARIAH • WEINBERG • JULIET TAYLOR • DR. ROSEN • FALCARO • BLANK • ROSS • DIAZ • SUSSMAN • CRAFA • ROSEN • COPA • COOPER • SCHLEIN • GALANTE • SUAREZ • BLOOM • JOE CICCONE • MATT DILLON • JULIE BUDD • JENNIFER GREY • PAROTTA • O'CALLAHAN • DeROSA • JUDGE BARRON • MEADOWS • GUILD • LOU CARVEL • MALCOLM THOMSON • TRAMAZZO • LINDA STACI • FRED SAMARONE • BERDIE ROBBINS • FRED DRASNER • JODY MILANO • JIMMY KING • EDDIE GERMANO • CHRISTY FERER • MICHAEL FUCHS • STANLEY DEUTSCH • DICK CLARK • CHUCK BARRIS • MR. PECK

INDEX

JOSEPH RAO

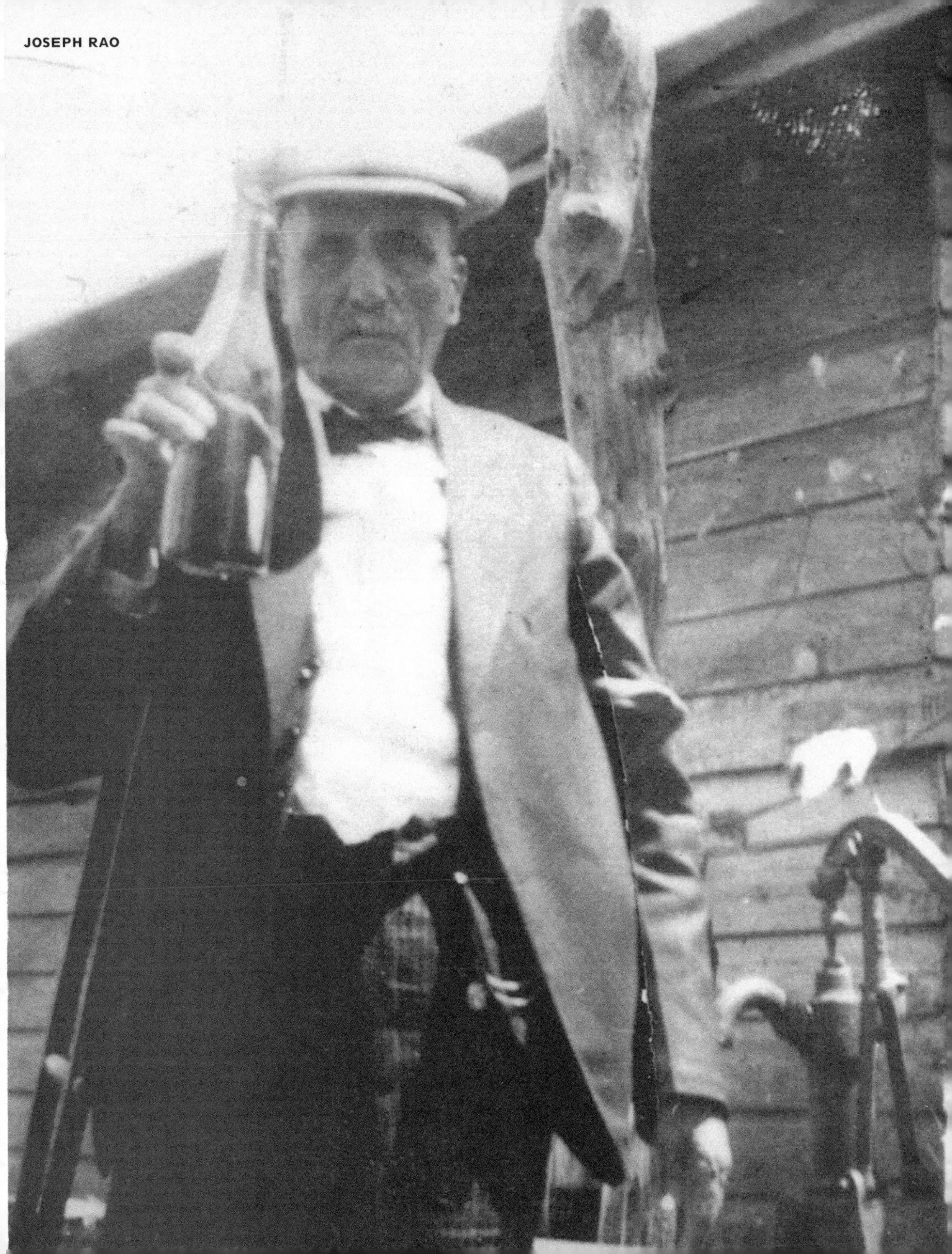

ABOUT THE AUTHOR

FRANK PELLEGRINO: Born in East Harlem, married with two children, founder and CEO of Rao's Specialty Foods, Inc.

www.raos.com
1–800–HOMEMADE